Flip the
S.W.I.T.C.H.

How to Turn On and
Turn Up Your Mindset

PJ McClure

ISBN: 978-0-9829833-0-0

*To Tammy, Ethan, and Avery for your unconditional support.
I love you beyond everything else.*

*To all of the amazing people, which have been a part of my
incredible journey into the minds of success. Your willingness
to answer my questions and share your lives changed my life
forever and continues to change the lives of millions through
this work.*

Most of us are imprisoned by something. We're living in darkness until something flips on the switch.
-Wynonna Judd

Table of Contents

Now that you've flipped the S.W.I.T.C.H.

Write your own

Foreword

You are about to invest the most precious, irreplaceable asset in the world... your time.

To make sure you get the most out of your investment, I have allowed the next few pages to be blank for your use. Instead of telling you what someone else got out of this book and how it changed his or her life, I invite you to begin your own story.

Think about your reason for reading this book. What do you hope you will get out of it? Write it down.

As you go through the book, come back here and make notes about your discoveries, the pages you found them on, and how they made you feel. When you're done, look through those notes and decide what you actually received. Write that down too.

The result will be your customized, one of a kind edition of Flip the S.W.I.T.C.H. with the foreword written by the person who knows you best... you.

This is only the beginning so enjoy the journey!

PJ McClure

What do you hope to get out of this book?

Don't forget to make references to page numbers as you go.

Chapter 1

Flipping the S.W.I.T.C.H.

Can it really be this easy?

The idea of flipping a switch to create success in life is entirely too simple for many people. They've bought into the notion that success is rare and therefore, must be difficult to attain. Or worse, that some people are just lucky or born into achievement and prosperity. Both notions are completely false and a big reason why so many don't bother to go for the gold in life.

I will grant you that achieving and maintaining major success requires work and a system. But that isn't the same as it being "hard."

Notice the distinction between just achieving success and achieving and maintaining success. Anyone can stumble into wealth, prosperity, and achievement. The real trick is sustaining those material riches along with health, happiness, and growth.

- Just ask 99% of lottery winners how hard it is to go from the outhouse to the penthouse and stay there.
- Ask 93% of second-generation millionaires why they fall into substance abuse, spend recklessly, and can't keep a relationship together.
- Why is the tragic, manic-depressive, child-star almost a proverb in our society?

These phenomena are the result of a lack of an internal support structure and we have more in common with them than maybe you realize.

The wealth and position placed upon these people is too heavy for their life and they have no way to withstand the pressure. They lack the perspective to understand what the money and popularity mean in the overall scheme of their life.

That missing internal support structure is the proper *mindset*. The guidance their mindset could provide would prevent them from wandering aimlessly. As it is, they are rudderless on the sea of life. Going whichever way the wind blows and panicking with every storm. Never sure where they will end up, crashing on the rocks, and always feeling like a victim.

This lack of internal guidance is what we often share with those that melt-down on the front page of the tabloids. The same thing keeps so many people broke financially and broken emotionally, only with less press. They look at those with money and happiness and think *those people* are somehow, special.

As humans, we want that same kind of **'special'** for our lives. We are innately wired to want more than we have, and we are not just talking about material things. We want more in terms of how we feed our souls.

When we let ourselves dream, we see a different life we would love to wake up to every day.

- A life that has everything, except financial stress.
- A life that gives us the ability to do what we love, when we want to do it.
- A life where we contribute more than we take and everyone appreciates what we have to offer.
- A life that blends our personal passions and professional expertise, seamlessly.
- A life of laughing easy and loving freely.
- And whether we use these exact words or not; a life of fulfillment, constant personal growth, and easy decisions.

With this dream in hand, we jump on a self-improvement book or max out our last credit card to attend a personal-development seminar.

The information we receive makes perfect sense. The motivation hit us right between the eyes and we're on fire to go achieve the life of which we dreamed. This is exactly what we needed! Now life is going to hand over the good stuff.

Then we step back into our current reality.

- The life we hate on Sunday night because it's ruled by financial stress.
- The life that has us so focused on making money that we don't even know what our personal passions are.
- The life of crying ourselves to sleep and neglecting our loved ones from stress.

- And whether we use these exact words or not; a life of denying our greatness, ignoring what's most important, and feeling hopeless to ever change.

With this kind of baggage around our necks, is it any wonder that we fall flat on our faces once the high of the book, seminar, or study-at-home program has worn off?

When the weight of our current reality comes crashing down in the form of family patterns, daily routines, and work expectations, we lack the basic foundation needed to hold up our dreams. Our mindset is not ready to support us in pursuit of those dreams so, they collapse.

This regression back into old patterns makes it easier to think that success is only meant for a few. Those special ones that seem to sail from day-to-day, collecting one personal success after another.

They set out after a goal and achieve it. The same adversities that send us into a tailspin don't seem to knock them off course at all.

The frustration that builds is stifling. Those people don't seem to be any more talented or intelligent than us. Many of them have backgrounds of pain and suffering that make our pasts seem like a walk in the park. How do they seemingly breeze through life and handle everything so well?

Every time we try to emulate their success, we find life making it impossible. Each day brings a new problem or roadblock for us battle and we forget all about having a new life. The daily trials leave us so mentally and emotionally exhausted, we can't keep pushing to make something better happen.

Still yet, you want to succeed. The dreams are still real. You can almost taste a better life. You've seen and tasted enough of what is possible that the instinctive desire to have more fulfillment will not go away.

It must be like the desire early humans had for light when the sun went down. They knew what it was like to see clearly in the light, so they had a desire to have light when it was not present. They just didn't know how to make it happen.

Think of your quest for more life in the same way. You have experienced flashes of your brilliance. You know that there is more within you to bring out. The desire is strong enough that your very being aches for more.

Just like those early humans, you have developed awareness, if only on a different level. Their awareness was that light is good. They could see clearly in the light, which enabled them to function with more confidence and protect themselves from predators. They reasoned more light could keep them alive.

Your awareness tells you those moments of brilliance make you feel alive and further enlightenment can make you more alive. You see the same aliveness in the successful people you yearn to imitate, but the way forward seems blocked.

I have good news and bad news. The bad news is I'm going to confirm your deepest fear. There is, without a doubt, a difference between the successful examples and you. I have interviewed, studied, and coached thousands to uncover and understand the difference and it is undeniable.

The good news is the difference is easily learned and you have complete control over every aspect that makes the difference. All you need is deeper awareness and a little instruction. What seems like an ocean of difference now will seem like no more than a small stream when we are finished.

Yes, you will still need to cross on your own, but I will show you each of the stepping-stones along the way.

More than anything else right now, I want you to take heart in knowing your desires are not foolish. The yearning and dreaming is your first clue to unraveling the mystery. Without the desire to have more in your life, there is no reason to seek, know, or learn. Nurture your desire.

That desire of early human's gave birth to harnessing the spark and turning it into fire. Then from fire to electricity. From electricity to light bulbs. Now our desires continue to reveal ways of getting more light out of less energy.

Largely, the population now takes for granted the ability to reach out our hands and flip a switch to replace darkness with light. We solve the problem of darkness with what seems like a very simple solution. After all, *it's only a switch.*

But that switch represents a complex and powerful system that generates electricity and carries it to your home.

The wiring that brings the electricity from outside your home to the bulb in the lamp is complex enough to make your head swim. All planned and implemented so that you and I can just reach out our hand and have what we want.

What if I told you that we can handle achieving success *the exact same way?*

With a little concentrated effort on your part, solving your life's issues and living life on your terms is as simple as flipping a switch.

Just like with electricity and the bulb, there is already a complex and powerful system in place to create and deliver your personal power. Our job here is to turn it on.

This isn't some mystical, 2,000-year-old secret that was discovered in a tomb and translated from a lost language.

We aren't going to expose an elite conspiracy of the world's rich and powerful to keep you down.

Nothing in this book requires you to vibrate at a certain frequency so your heart's desires can come vibrating down the road toward you.

The tools you are about to learn are all contained in the only vessel that you have complete and total control of... *yourself.*

Everything you learn here takes advantage of how your mind is already wired. In fact, each tool is already in motion in your life and only requires simple adjustments to make it all work for you.

Eventually, the tools become a system and that system is the key to long-term success. The system is your mindset.

With this system in full swing, the basics of achievement become automatic. The same things that you once envied in others show up for you as a rule. The frustrations that used to stress you out, melt away because your mindset takes care of them for you.

All of the energy you used to expend dealing with all of the problems life threw your way is now spent taking advantage of the opportunities you find on a daily basis instead.

Just as you turn on a light without giving a second thought to the vast and complex energy grid that delivers electricity, you will begin to turn on your own personal mindset without concern for how it arrived at your fingertips.

With all of the former stumbling blocks turned in to stepping-stones, you can focus your energy on the larger life you've always wanted.

When we are finished, you will have an understanding of success, happiness, and fulfillment that allows you to have anything you truly want. You will know what you want, why you want it, and how to get it. Life will seem different and your approach to everything improves.

I make these statements and promises against the backdrop of my own experience and the lives I have seen transformed. Through the diligent and faithful application of these principles, your mindset becomes a willing ally in the daily pursuit of your dreams.

Still not sure how this system can deliver? Let me share one of the stories from my own life of this system in action.

My yesterdays were burned by Phoenix fire

Yet in the death's ash, embers of hope remain

New dreams given birth in despair

Covered with ash, I mourn what was

To remember what will be no more

Then like the Phoenix I'll rise

With renewed passion glowing red, yellow, orange

Ash will give way to flame

Like the Phoenix I'll soar again

Amy Sondova

Atypicalgirl.wordpress.com

Chapter 2

The House that Fire Built

Burning

"We have a fire!"

I struggled to wake from my Nyquil induced sleep. *"We what...?"*

"We have a fire!" my wife said with enough emotion to bring me around.

I hopped out of bed and stumbled toward some unusual noises in the garage. When I opened the door, the heat from 100 holiday ovens hit me in the face and an ominous, orange pulse lit the smoke filled garage.

Slamming the door, I yelled to my wife to grab the kids and call 911. She got our 4-year-old daughter, I grabbed our 6-year-old son, and we hit the door.

Our bathrobe-clad neighbor was coming across the yard with his cell phone in-hand. He had emergency services on the phone and helped us across to his house.

Making sure everyone was safe in his kitchen; I went back outside to survey the situation.

Earlier in the day I had driven 11 hours straight to get back home from a business trip. My son's first-grade class was reciting the pledge of allegiance before the school board meeting and I wanted to be there. I missed the pledge, but felt good to be home.

My trip had awarded me with a two new accounts and wicked head cold. The kind of cold that can put you down for a couple of days. So before going to bed I took a dose of Nyquil... *the nighttime, sniffling, sneezing, coughing, achy head, knock your butt out, so you can rest medicine...* with the plan of sleeping in and feeling better.

Now as I stood in my neighbor's yard at 2:30am, with soaking wet feet and thanking God my wife is a light sleeper, my head cold was the furthest thing from my mind.

I watched our garage door, cycling up and down uncontrollably, reveal and conceal the blaze consuming two cars, a riding lawn mower, every tool, and piece of recreation equipment we owned.

Within seconds, small plumes of flame burst through the roof in numerous places. The fire was already in the attic and apparently burning above our heads when my wife woke up. Had she slept for a few minutes more, none of us would have woken up.

The fire department arrived in a reasonable amount of time and got to work to see what they could save. By 3:30am, it was apparent their efforts had turned from save-a-home to training drills. At 8:30am, they began rolling up hoses and filling out paperwork.

A firefighter doing his best to "cool" the blaze
because they couldn't put it out.

Over 6 hours, 20 fire fighters, and 31,000 gallons of water later... we had our lives, our pajamas, and an overwhelming sense of gratitude.

Our son captured the overall attitude of our family when the whole episode was less than 30 minutes old. I went into our neighbor's house after the fire department arrived and told my wife we would likely lose everything. I glanced over her shoulder to my son and watched him for a moment as he considered what those words meant.

He looked over at his sister and said, *"Oh well, it's just stuff and we can always get more of it. All of us are safe and daddy still has a job,"* then turning to his mother, *"Can I go back to sleep now?"*

His biggest concern of the entire night was, were we going to make him go to school in his pajamas.

Gratitude ran deep and more things for which to be grateful arrived in droves. Before the sun had come up and the fire had died, we had people from our community rallying around us.

Clothes showed up for our kids, collections were taken up and delivered, and offers for any kind of help we needed streamed in. During the rest of the morning the kids gave tours of 'what used to be' while we dealt with our insurance company and secured a place for us to live.

As word got around during the next few days, family and friends showed up or called. This was when it became obvious to me who knew us well and who did not.

Everyone was well meaning and sincere. They all had great concern and compassion for our situation, but not all of them really understood where our heads were.

People wanted to comfort and cheer us up. They showed up with their best *"happy faces"* on, expecting to do their part to pull us through and soon realized *we were already through.* As a family, we were moving forward and making plans for where we wanted to go next. Life had not stopped and neither had we.

Those who knew us well realized we were on the move and everything was fine. Yes, we would need some help from time-to-time, but wasting concern over whether we would be okay or not was not necessary.

Those who did not know us had distinctly different reactions. In fact, they seemed a little disappointed we were not devastated and kept trying to talk us into feeling bad.

"Why aren't you more upset?"

"It just hasn't sank in, has it?"

"Oh, you must be in shock."

Shock?! Really? When you stand in your neighbor's yard at 3:00 in the morning and watch every material possession you have worked for burn, shock floats away with the smoke. Reality brings its full weight to the party.

When your kids take their grandma by the hand and lead her over to the side of the house, which used to be their bedrooms, you wonder what will happen. Then they point to charred and soaked remains of their favorite toy or stuffed animal and say, *"I'm sad it's gone, but I'm really glad I wasn't in there with it,"* you realize they have a strong grip on reality. Shock is not part of the equation.

The thing that amazed most people was how we did not take or require any significant time to recover and get ahead. Even if shock would have entered in, I am not sure the results would have been any different.

"How can you make such bold and confident strides this soon after a disaster?"

"Aren't you worried about making a bad decision?"

The truth is, no. We were not worried about making bad decisions because we were not making any decisions. Our mindset as a family had taken over and we were effectively operating on autopilot. We had flipped a switch.

As you come to understand throughout this book, there were not any decisions to make because the way forward was obvious.

With all of the distractions and options in the moment, our mindset brought the best option for us into focus. We considered circumstances, looked at the options, and moved to the obvious answer.

It was easier after the fire because of the simple and effective work we had done prior. The same mindset, which was building a continually improving life when things were normal took over and continued improving our life after the fire.

That is another important distinction. At no time were we concentrating on getting back to where we were before the fire. At all times we were trying to get ahead of where we had been.

The rest of the world was not going to tread water and wait for us regardless of how stressful an event might be. Life does not wait. The ten months prior to fire had given us plenty of chances to understand how important it is to keep moving forward.

Starting with the first of the year, I had made a major job change. As the sole breadwinner, anything that affects my income is a big deal. This new job could provide a big boost in income, but it was all dependent on earning commissions in an industry I knew nothing about. This change alone is enough to rank at the top of most; *"Things I did this year"* lists.

Later, in May, I got a call from my wife's cell phone. Expecting news about dinner or plans for the weekend, I answered in my low, sexy voice. *"Hello baby."* Instead of my wife laughing at me like she always does, I heard my mom's nervous words.

"Um, honey? Everything is okay, but Tammy had a heart-attack."

I left work and made the 30-minute drive to the hospital in a bit of a daze. Admittedly, shock was present. My wife, Tammy, was only 39 years-old at the time and a heart attack caught me off guard.

Broken leg, burnt herself, or some other physical injury I could have taken in-stride, but a heart-attack...

Over the course of the next five days in the hospital, we learned she had a *spontaneous dissection of the arterial wall*. The interior wall of one of her arteries peeled away from the rest and collapsed like wet wallpaper. The same thing killed actor, John Ritter, except his was in the aorta and hers was in a less critical area.

You prepare yourself for many things in life. That is not one of them. I spent the five days in the hospital with her. We laughed to ourselves, visited with friends and family, and talked about how fortunate we were.

During the course of all of these other activities, I was finishing my bachelor degree as a full-time, non-traditional student. In other words, working full-time and schooling full-time. I completed those requirements in August and moved immediately into a full-time masters program.

Had it not been for our mindset as a family, I would have bailed on school more than once. The encouragement of my wife and kids made the goal of completion an integrated part of our family experience.

The stress my classmates were experiencing made me appreciate how we operated even more. The difficulties they expressed about keeping their family life together or keeping up with homework in the face of a demanding career reminded me of the importance of a strong mindset.

Take all of the things happening during that 10-month period and throw in a total-loss house fire on a chilly October night. By most standards, we had enough stress and yuck to warrant a time-out. No one would have blamed us if we took a few months to checkout and float along.

Shutting down never showed up as a favorable option. Though slightly different and decidedly inconvenienced, we continued along our path. We might have lost our material possessions, but we did not lose who we are as people.

The life we lived before, during, and after the hardships I have outlined were not that different from one another. We stayed focused and true to what matters to us as a family and, as you will see, kept right on rolling along.

Chapter 3

The House that Fire Built

Rising

One of our major joys as a family is travel. So for Thanksgiving a few weeks later, my wife and I, with four of our closest friends, went from Missouri to Florida for the week.

It might have been easier to cancel the trip, but we were able to enrich our lives on numerous levels by going.

Since we were now living in the basement of our neighbor down the road, we decided to travel for Christmas.

Through my grandparent's generosity and our ability to make quick decisions, we booked a week at an amazing wilderness lodge over Christmas.

It felt like being dropped into Christmas village. Cabins lined the lakeside with wisps of smoke curling out of their chimneys. Horse-drawn carriages and nightly wagon rides rolled straight out of a Currier and Ives print.

There was a workshop where the kids could build toys with Santa and the elves. More importantly, our minds were on what was possible in life, not on what had happened.

That holiday season was one many people can only dream of when things are good. The idea of such a stretch during a perceived time of hardship and stress is unheard of. Still yet, we had it.

Our babies in front of the lodge's Christmas tree.

And I do not tell you any part of the story to impress you, *but to impress upon you,* this kind of life is available to everyone.

Not just the material things of beaches and resorts, but also the emotional and intellectual aspects of fulfillment and progress.

Deciding to provide experiences for those you love and adding to your own life as well. All of this is a matter of choice and a function of mindset.

How do you choose to go through life? What do you want out of this one, irreplaceable life? Will you make things happen or allow them happen to you?

The biggest thing I want to you see at this point is you need a conscious means of operating in life. A philosophy. A plan.

This can start within you as an individual or you can be a part of the operating philosophy of a group, like your family. Either way, the experience of knowing why and how you approach life is transforming.

You become someone others marvel because of how you move. They see adversity, you see opportunity. They wonder why you aren't frozen with indecision and fear. You see the next step as obvious and eagerly take it with a sense of adventure and anticipation.

The day after the house burned, the kids went to spend a couple of days with a grandma while my wife and I got things moving. We sat down at a local restaurant to put some thoughts on paper about what necessities we lacked, but our conversation quickly turned to a bigger matter: what kind of house we were going to build. And how it would serve our life

We were not sure when the insurance company's investigation would end or even how much of a settlement we would receive. Somehow, none of it slowed us down. Furthermore, we did not discuss what we had before. We talked about what we wanted.

What rooms and what size were the main questions we answered. Details were for another time.

A couple of days later I bought a computer program, which made creating a house plan pretty easy. I decided to use the same footprint as our old house and began laying out rooms.

Everything we wanted would not fit on one floor, so I added another. *"What's the big deal,"* I thought, *"it isn't going to cost anymore for two floors while it's in the computer."*

The most important part of beginning the drawing process was it helped us form our vision.

I showed my wife as it progressed and got her thoughts. The kids saw their rooms and began decorating them in their heads and drew pictures of where their furniture would go.

Our conversations revolved around, *"when we're in our new house,"* and we all knew it was only a matter of time.

With this vision crystallizing in our minds, I should mention, I had no idea how we were going to build it.

All totaled, the house I drew was three times bigger than what we lost. The materials were nicer, the craftsmanship would need to be better, and we still did not have an insurance settlement.

Knowing all of this, we kept checking *"reality"* against our vision. At no time did we feel we needed to shrink from what we saw for our family. We intended to build that house and this is where people on the outside would say, *"things started getting weird."*

Our settlement came in below what we had hoped. Moreover, they expected us to reuse some of the walls, which had the tops burnt off, and the floor, which had received 31,000 gallons of water and hours of smoke. I arm-wrestled with the adjustor over these matters and lost. So we smiled, took our check, and got to work.

By all contractor estimates, the house we wanted to build would cost two and half times our settlement and a year to complete because of how difficult it is to build during Missouri winters.

We were willing to put some cash toward it, but not much. I've got some background in construction and really believed, if we could get the right general contractor on the job, we could make it happen for much less.

Not to mention my vision of the house included hosting Thanksgiving dinner in less than a year. There had to be a way to get it done.

The contractor I wanted on the job also happened to be a good friend. Unfortunately, I knew he and his crew were several hundred miles away in Louisiana working on jobs from hurricane damage. Regardless, I felt like I should give him a call for advice.

It turned out he and the crew had a break in the action in Louisiana. They were headed to within 35 miles of us to take care of a new contract and would be looking for work within three weeks.

I shared my plans with him and we struck a deal that kept his crew working and got our house off the ground.

The economy had knocked the wind out of our local building industry. We were told this would actually add to our difficulty because many people had taken other jobs or traveled out of the area to find work. We kept going.

I called a local concrete specialist who I had met the year before when our sons played basketball together. He took a look and confirmed we could use the same foundation as our old house with a couple of modifications, as long as the cleanup was done correctly.

Thinking I would do all of the cleanup, with the aid of volunteer help, I asked him how he needed it done. Instead, he said he was slow for the next couple of weeks and offered to do it as part of the bid to modify the foundation.

My contractor's foreman told me about his brother, the electrician. With me doing the grunt work for him over a few weekends, he put our wiring together for 26% of our anticipated cost.

We never asked for a better deal or sympathy from anyone. They all offered the best they could because they needed the work.

Cabinets and counter tops, hardwood floors and custom tile work, all of it was better quality than we expected and all of it at discounts we would not have dreamed.

Our original intent was to use a combination of vinyl and wood siding to finish the house. We wanted brick and stone, but did not see how we could make it happen within the budget. We decided to do what we could to prepare the house for brick later down the road, so I called my stepfather who is a brick mason.

"What kind of brick were you thinking of using?" he asked.

"I don't know," I replied. *"We hadn't really gotten that far because we aren't ready to buy it."*

"If you want to take a look, my friend ordered a bunch of brick for a commercial job and the customer didn't like it," he said matter-of-factly. *"Now he's stuck with it and would probably make you a good deal on it."*

Before we could go look at this rejected brick, a random guy showed up at the house site. He introduced himself and asked if we were planning to put brick on the house.

He and his crew needed work to get through winter and he offered me a rate to install brick, which really did not mean anything to me. I wrote it down, thanked him for stopping by, and said I would call him if we liked the brick we were looking at.

If we had shopped for months to find the perfect brick, we would not have chosen what we saw in the rejected brick. Fortunately, we did not get to shop and the brick could not have been more perfect.

We asked for a price and he gave it to us at a cost, which made it only 5% more than I had planned to pay for vinyl siding.

I asked my stepfather about the crew and told him the rate they offered. *"He does great work and that rate is unreal."* In total, we increased the value of the house by more than 15% and spent less than 6% more to do it.

That's good math and it is all because we had a mindset, which guided us from one opportunity to the next.

The cleanup started during the second week of December and we moved in during the third week of July. Our total cost ended at less than half of what we were told to expect and Thanksgiving dinner was amazing.

Why does any of this matter to you?

Life is impartial. It rains on the good and the bad. Opportunities are presented to the financially rich and the poor. Our lives, and I mean all of us, are made of two separate components, which combine to make our experiences. Events and meaning.

Events are the things that happen. Birth, death, marriage, divorce, getting a job, losing a job. All of these things are events.

They are not good or bad by themselves. They are only events. The meaning we give to the events is what determines the negative or positive effect it has on our lives.

The previous story of significant change, health issues, and loss of property is nothing more than a series of events. Would it be safe to say, different people would react in different ways to each of those events?

Yes, they would all assign a different meaning. Why?

If the events are the exact same, why would it mean something different from one person to the next?

Why would one person be paralyzed with fear or racked with depression over an event, while another comes out the other side bigger and better than they went in?

How is it, a few of the people you know always seem to *"fall into"* great situations while others constantly struggle just to get by?

The answer is *mindset.*

How you can understand and take control of your mindset is the subject of the following chapters. The information you get here took me 12 years of dedicated effort to discover and only an instant to realize its value.

With a few simple choices, I built a mindset, which took 25 years of unguided, destructive behaviors and turned them into a lifetime of possibility. Are you ready to make it happen for you?

Chapter 4

Time To Build Yours

What is a mindset?

The textbook definition says mindset is:

A fixed mental attitude or disposition
that predetermines a person's responses to and
interpretations of situations.

...ok... so my mindset determines how I see and operate in the world. That's easy enough to understand. But it only tells me what mindset means... not what makes it.

When I first came face-to-face with the concept of mindset, I was frustrated beyond belief. I had found my way into a financial services organization that focused heavily on personal development.

In my mid-twenties at the time, I had no previous exposure to self-improvement and had always gotten along on guts, luck, and talent. The idea of consciously guiding my life to a destination of my choosing blew me away.

I devoured every tape and book they put in my hands. It all made so much sense.

- How to set goals.

- Why my attitude had such an impact on my accomplishments.

- The qualities effective leaders have, which causes others to follow.

Everything pointed toward success. It all looked so good, I felt like success was assured. I only needed to take the same steps as those people I admired and I could enjoy the same life. I took off like a rocket.

Maybe it was because I had so much room to grow or maybe I really made remarkable strides, but I began to have success like I had never experienced. Money, promotions, and status within the company came running at me. Leaders in the company began including me in their inner circles and my peers asked me to lead trainings about getting ahead.

Then, without any apparent warning, I crashed.

Things stopped happening and my income plummeted. Always the competitor, I reapplied myself by ratcheting up my regimen of tapes, books, and seminars. Bigger goals and more public-accountability seemed to get me going again.

I forced a smile on lousy days and laughed especially hard on the good ones. When my production numbers picked up, I stepped to the front of the room and cheered everyone on. When they tanked, I kept quiet and acted like things were cool.

I have never experienced such an empty feeling in all of my life.

It is no wonder; the next crash came just as hard as the first. The major difference this time was I now had the additional baggage of failure.

I looked around at my peers and the leaders I followed to see what I was missing. What I found during this conscious look both disturbed and motivated me.

Of all the people I knew well, most were having the same experience as me. Rise and fall. Start and stall. They did not give me any indication they were doing anything differently. This was the disturbing part.

The motivating part was a few of the people I knew where taking the material and building an amazing life. Their rise might not have been meteoric, but they didn't fall. Every book or seminar gave them a new tool, which took them even higher.

When life gave them adversity, you might not even know something happened. Not because they were in denial or went delusional. They just handled it and went on. Stronger and better than before.

What was the difference? I didn't know but vowed to find out. It was the only chance I had of getting off the emotional roller coaster that was wearing me out.

Not knowing where else to start, I asked all of the successful people I had access to, what they were doing. I got a smattering of different answers and they all sounded like motivational tapes.

Aside from a couple of insightful comments about internal motivation, everything seemed like the same things I had done. I didn't notice anything unique.

Next, I asked the company leaders I could access. As they reflected on their own success and the prowess of the few people I used as examples, they began to use a certain word repeatedly. *Mindset.*

"I've always had the mindset that no matter what, I was going to be successful."

"Her mindset puts her ahead of the game before it even starts."

"The reason he can bounce back quicker than everyone around him is his mindset."

On and on they rolled the word around. It took a while, but I finally recognized the pattern. *"It's obvious,"* I thought. *"Successful people have a certain mindset, which makes it all happen."* That is when I found the textbook definition of mindset from the opening of this chapter.

...how I see the world and operate in it....

Feeling as if I had found the keystone to unrealized success and prosperity, I went back to those leaders who had led me to the water and said, *"I understand now, mindset is the difference. So will you please tell me what a mindset is made of and how I get the one I want?"*

It seemed like a reasonable request until it became obvious, they didn't know. In fact, I'm not sure if any of them had ever considered the questions at all.

Some of them were amused at how stumped they were and some were a little upset with me for asking the question.

"What do you mean, what is a mindset made of? Isn't it obvious?"

"No. That's why I'm asking."

Each one of them did their best to answer and only managed an extended version of what the proper mindset does for a successful person. A few dismissed the questions entirely, but most finally admitted they had no idea how to answer.

I had at least piqued their interest and they offered to help me figure it out if they could.

As leaders in a large company, most of them had access to the motivational and success gurus of the day. These people spent their lives in the business of creating successful people so it made sense they would know the answer to such a vital question.

I went to the seminars and got access to the presenter through my now growing network. As soon as I could, I would ask the question.

"What makes a mindset and how do I get the one I want?"

All of the answers were a variation of the textbook definition. None of them provided any real guidance toward how to make this all-important piece of my life work for me.

I got responses like,

"The successful entrepreneur has a mindset, which helps them recognize opportunities and risks to make them successful."

"Great leaders have a mindset that keeps their approach to leadership in line with the things that are most important to them."

"The mindset of top-notch executives gives them the advantage of knowing what decisions will take their company and careers to new levels."

"Leaders respond to adversity in a productive way because their mindset is bent that way."

All great answers from wonderful people *and all completely useless* when it came to helping me know what to do. They were not intentionally vague, but their answers made it even more apparent, this was not a topic with vast understanding.

Superficial examples of what a mindset does really do not provide any instruction as to what a mindset *IS*. So I refined and renewed my quest.

Find out what makes a mindset and determine what makes it work better for some than others. In particular, is it possible that a mindset is learn-able or is it something you are born with?

I began having conversations with the most successful people I could find. People with obvious financial success were the first targets.

Through the influential people who were now sympathetic to my cause, I reached out to a Fortune 20 CEO and five more in the Fortune 500. Numerous small business owners and world-class salespeople.

Some of them proved exactly what they seemed, successful in every way. They had financial abundance, good health, great relationships, spiritually centered, and always looking to contribute to others. Their insights were priceless and shaped the basis of my work today. These became group A.

They answered every question and gave as freely of their time as they could. By giving me access to their network, I learned more than I ever could. It turns out; they were just as interested to know the answers as I was.

There was an entirely different side to the first group I gained access to as well. Though all of them were unquestionably financial successes, not all of them had everything else going for them. A few had nothing but money.

Their health was shot, their relationships were hollow, and they had no spiritual sense about them. This group helped to redefine what I considered a successful person.

Some of them were sad and the others hardened. Only a couple seemed the least bit interested in what I was doing and still yet, my experiences with them had as much to do with shaping my work as group A.

Comparing my notes from each group, I saw there was as much information in what B was missing as there was in what A possessed. I took this new, more expansive definition of success and actually shrank the criteria for inclusion into the two groups.

A million dollar net worth was no longer important. I was learning financial abundance means something different to many people. Habits of personal growth and fulfillment were absolutely essential to all of the members of group A, though they might have called them something different.

Healthy body and relationships were integral, but each of them defined those a little differently. I was not really sure where all of this was headed, but I knew I couldn't turn back now.

While I felt my way around this new territory, something unexpected began to happen. People with the same frustrations and fears I had, started coming to me for help. My little, closet-like office always seemed to have someone popping by to chat. They would say things like,

"I can't seem to keep any momentum once I've started after a goal."

"What can I do to have more confidence in my decisions?"

"I'm stuck and can't seem to get motivated to start moving again."

"My career is killing my personal life and I don't know what to do." Or

"My personal life is killing my career and I don't know what to do."

Any of those sound familiar? The part that baffled me about being asked these questions was, *I didn't have the answers either*. My struggles were the same as theirs... or so I thought.

What they saw in me was a change. During my search, I was steadily becoming a different person and they wanted to experience that difference for themselves.

My new perspective attracted people. I kept using my access to the successful people I interviewed and wove the frustrations of everyone else into my research. I have to admit, I liked trying to help. It provided a little bit of a rush and turned my originally selfish reasons into a bigger cause.

Over the course of the next eight years, I continued to meet with anyone who would give me the time. I added 246 more to group A and over 700 to group B.

They granted me time over breakfast, a quick lunch, or a beer. Sometimes at trade-shows or conventions. I drove several to and from airports or volunteered to work at their events.

After 1,000's of hours, more than 1,600 interviews and coaching sessions, and no less than 1,200,000 calories… I found what I was looking for.

All of the different answers and techniques, which I was originally told were part of a successful person's arsenal, were not always there for group A. Of all of the traits, which are supposed to be keys to success, I could not pick one that was common among everyone. Group B showed more consistency in those supposed success traits than group A.

After hours of mind mapping and reams of notebook paper, I managed to distill all of my notes into six distinct categories. No matter how hard I tried, these six would not breakdown any further. They were not the products of anything else. Everything else came from them. They were:

- Purpose

- Belief

- Vision

- Action

- Gratitude

- Forgiveness

Every person from group A had these six elements working for them in their lives. They might not have been consciously practicing each, but it was a part of their foundational mindset.

It became obvious; this was missing for the members of group B. Every one of them was missing one or more of these six elements.

What was most encouraging to me, and the members of group B, as I shared my theory, is each of these six is completely within the control of the individual. I began to call them, **The Elements of Personal Choice**, because each of these is already in your life and you have a *choice* of whether or not the element serves or hinders you.

These choices are how you form your mindset. The members of group A had a certain way of doing things, which put their mindset in place for them. Some of the things they did consciously and some were a product of their upbringing or environment.

One of them learned about purpose from her instructor at Yale, another learned purpose in a Singapore slum. Background did not matter. It was their choices bringing everything together to form their mindset.

What matters most about mindset as we get started?

It is important to understand, mindset does not have an on-off switch... it is always on. The difference is whether we are conscious of its presence and role in our lives. If we go back to the textbook definition of mindset,

> *A fixed mental attitude or disposition that predetermines a person's responses to and interpretations of situations*

We see mindset is predetermined and dictates how we respond to situations. I agree with most of the textbook definition, but it will help you if we tweak it to reflect what I have found.

> *Mindset is the programmable, subconscious framework, which filters input so the conscious mind can respond.*

Sorry if that got a little wordy... let's break it down.

Programmable – your mindset is NOT fixed. You have full control and authority to make it whatever you choose. You tell your mindset what you want and it has no choice but to give it to you.

Subconscious framework – mindset operates on the same level as breathing. While you are going about your day, how often do you actually "think" about breathing?

However, as soon as I mention breathing, you realize you can take control and affect it. Your mindset operates automatically based on the previous information you've given *and* you can consciously take control to give it new information.

Filters input – We receive millions (maybe billions) of bits of input every day. So much in fact, our conscious minds start to tune-out when we try to take in too much.

That reaction is the *zoning out* effect, which has happened to us all. Your mindset acts as a filter and only lets through what your conscious (thinking) mind needs to function and respond.

By handling all of the noise of the world on a subconscious level, your mindset frees your conscious mind to concentrate on the things you value and deem important to your life.

Think of this example.

You are at a party and there is typical party noise. Conversations everywhere, music, and so on. While engaged in a conversation with someone… you hear your name mentioned by someone else, in another conversation, across the room! How and why?

It was not that the people were not talking before. It is not likely everything in the room went silent just as they spoke your name.

You heard it because we have trained our minds to know, our names are very important. Your subconscious mind was working overtime to filter out all of the input in the room (other conversations, music, lighting, temperature, bad dancing, etc.) so you could focus on your conversation. In the stream of those thousands of bits of blocked input, your name got through.

The subconscious knew this piece was important. More important than all of the rest... so it gave that particular piece of input to your conscious mind for response.

This is mindset in action.

I hope you are beginning to see, these things happen all the time. Billions of pieces of input, only a few get through. Now the trick becomes designing your mindset, your filter, to let through the things to help design your best life.

And I really mean, your entire life. This not confined to work or home. This is not a one-dimensional strategy like time-management, goal setting, or better relationships. Taking conscious control of your mindset improves every area of your life. It is automatic.

As you bring your mindset into alignment, you make the best use of your time and enjoy each moment. Goal setting turns into goal achieving because you have stacked the deck in your favor. You see ways to have and improve your ideal relationships. And on and on...

You are about to learn how to flip the S.W.I.T.C.H., and your entire approach to life will change and improve. Before, a set of circumstances might have shown you nothing but adversity and problems.

When you flip the S.W.I.T.C.H and turn on your personal mindset to work *for you,* you will see opportunities and new ways to be happy and productive.

Most importantly, what you learn here will serve you for the rest of your life. This system continues to answer every question my clients and I have about life.

In fact, the most commonly asked questions guided my research and journey that brought us both here. You might recognize some of the questions I started with as your own.

Chapter 5

Time to Build Yours

The Questions that Needed Answers

The previous five hours left me drained and exhilarated, all at the same time.

The office I worked in held training on Saturday mornings for all of the personal financial advisers in our area. They covered new products, prospecting and sales techniques, and personal growth strategies.

When you were on top of your game and producing big numbers, you were asked to conduct a training topic.

My recent numbers were enough to get some attention, so on a whim; I asked the regional vice president if I could have a separate training afterward to share some things I had learned about success.

"I'll only need an hour," I assured him.

He put it up for vote and all of the officers agreed to let me.

During the past year, I had begun to develop a reputation for the passion and insight I brought to my speaking opportunities. It was no secret that I had buried myself in studying successful people and I think they were curious to see what I had to say. Besides, it wasn't likely that anyone would stick around that long on a Saturday afternoon anyway.

My division manager and good friend Casey helped me pull my resources together. By the time we outlined everything I wanted to cover, there was *over three hours of material*. Seeing no way to cut it down and still have the desired effect, Casey offered the kind of sage advice I had come to expect.

"Screw it. The worst that can happen is they'll leave."

On that Thursday I pulled together all of my notes on what I had come to understand about the first element of personal choice, purpose. I built a workbook, practiced my presentation, and slept for maybe two hours during the next two days. This training was more than a chance to share some findings.

For the previous six months, I had spent more time counseling my peers on matters of personal growth than on building financial portfolios. Product sales were leaving me cold, but the rush of helping someone through a tough spot was nothing I had ever experienced.

No one, including me, thought that I had all of the answers. I knew that I had way more questions than answers. But people still repeatedly sought me out to coach them along.

I had to find out if I could bring value to a group and hold my own in front of a room. Could I build a life helping others get better while I did the same thing?

Word had gotten around that I was offering a special session after the normal training and reps that didn't normally come on Saturday mornings rolled in to see what was going on. On an average morning, we would have 20-25 people attend. When we dismissed at noon that day, there were 60.

The VP asked how many were staying for the additional training and everyone raised his or her hand. Four of them asked if it would be okay if their spouses joined us. When the group broke for a 30-minute lunch, Casey and I sprinted for the copy shop up the street to make 44 more workbooks.

Nervous as I had ever been, we passed out workbooks at 12:40; I put my watch in my pocket and started.

I truthfully do not remember everything about that afternoon. There are patches of total lucidity and blurs that seemed like a trance. I made conscious eye contact with every person in that room at one point or another.

They responded to every point and nodded with understanding when I revealed a hard truth. They stopped me and asked questions for which I didn't always have an answer. That seemed to be okay with everyone.

No one left and a few of them cried. I think there was a bathroom break in there as well, but I couldn't swear to it.

When I turned the last page of my workbook and realized that I was done, it was 5:26. I asked them all to fill out the little survey in their workbook, smiled, and thanked them all for staying and making this a great day for me. It was my first and still the most special standing ovation.

By the time I finished talking to everyone afterward it was almost 7:00. I jumped in Casey's car and we were buzzing about the day the whole way to his apartment.

"I feel kind of bad that it took so long," I said, not really sure if I meant it.

"Are you kidding," Casey laughed as he almost drove off the road. *"That was incredible! I've never seen you so tuned in."*

"You mean that, right?" I wanted to believe it but didn't want to set myself up to look like a jerk.

"Of course I do. But don't believe me. What do those surveys say?"

I hadn't taken any time to look at the fist-full of yellow cards. At that moment, I still couldn't look and told some lie about getting sick if I read in a car. Casey chuckled and gunned it.

After a couple of beers, I wandered by the table where I had dropped the cards. Trying unsuccessfully to look casual, I read the top few.

"Wow PJ! I feel like I'm better prepared for success than I've ever been before."

"I've struggled with finding meaning for years. Your presentation broke it all down to a level that really made sense to me. Thanks."

62 of the 64 cards had responses that ranged from glowing praise to mentions of being anointed. The other two hated me and expressed that I was entirely too personal and made them uncomfortable. I couldn't have been happier.

There was absolutely no middle ground in the way people responded and that was all the validation I needed to know that I was on to something.

While it's true that I read the remarks over-and-over that night, the cards had something that was much more valuable in the long run. In the moment of wrapping up the presentation and explaining about the response cards, I asked everyone to do something I hadn't planned on.

"If there are any questions that are troubling you right now, write them down on the back."

I didn't know if it would be helpful for anyone, but it seemed like the right thing to do at the time. 58 people took me up on the offer and spelled out what was keeping them awake at night. Even one of the two that thought I stunk wrote a heartfelt question on the back.

The responses were anonymous, but as I read them, I got a picture of each person and their struggle. It was easy because I had all of the same questions.

Taken as a group, the 58 questions could be boiled down to 13. More than 12 years later, my coaching clients and colleagues that I've worked with have had the same questions. Maybe you've got some of them too.

- Isn't desire enough?

- Why doesn't goal setting work for everyone?

- Can I really "fake it till I make it?"

- Can personal and financial success exist together?

- Why do similar people get such different results?

- Why do I fall back after making such progress?

- How do I know what I'm afraid of and make it go away?

- Why does my self-confidence fluctuate so much?

- I've failed before, why won't it happen again?

- Why can't I get rid of negative thoughts?

- How do I find my life's purpose?

- Why do I procrastinate?

- Is it really possible for anyone to be successful?

This isn't an exhaustive list of every question I've ever been asked, but these represent the most common and recurring.

If any of these belong to you, I want to establish a little understanding about the root of the question so that you can discover the solution as we go through the steps in this book.

The Questions

Isn't desire enough?

In a driven, type-A environment, the idea of "wanting something so bad you can taste it" is a prerequisite.

Any time that I found myself waning on a goal or lacking the motivation to move forward, my well-meaning mentors would tell me, *"You just don't want it bad enough."*

The notion of calling someone's level of desire into question seems completely ridiculous to me now. I had nights of crying myself to sleep and making myself sick with desire.

Convincing me that I could want success more than I did was pointless, but it did make me doubt my level of commitment. Though never tempted, I began to understand the emotional drama that could push someone toward suicide.

I firmly believe that you *"gotta wanna"* if you are ever going to accomplish anything. That said, just wanting something will never be enough to get it. Desire is a short-term emotion and disappears the instant things get challenging... unless there is something more substantial to back it up.

Why doesn't goal setting work for everyone?

Bad goals are a plague on society. People are constantly setting goals because that's what we are told to do. *"A famous Harvard study showed that successful people have goals."* No kidding…we needed Harvard for that?

Next, we hear that our goals must have a certain structure in order to accomplish them. The S.M.A.R.T. method is the most popular and is useful in structuring a goal, but it doesn't make them any more attainable by itself. If I have a bad goal, I can't make it smart enough to matter.

The acronym is broken down:

S –specific

M-measureable

A-attainable

R-realistic

T-timely

All great elements, but millions of people can attest, this alone does not help them achieve goals. Instead of worrying about the structure, maybe we should start deeper and first determine if the goal is something that we really want to achieve.

Traditional goal setting focuses in the wrong places. Goals are not where we start the road to achievement. They are a bi-product of a strong, functional mindset.

Can I really "fake it till I make it?"

Popular as it may be, the idea of acting as if you are something you are not, is psychotic. At least in terms of becoming successful. I cannot count the number of people, me included, that tried to put this notion into practice, only to end up more miserable than before.

"Tell yourself that you are successful and you'll be successful." I have to admit that the strategy worked for me… for about six minutes. Then the rest of the world, who apparently wasn't in on the gag, brought me screaming back to reality.

"What do you mean I'm broke and they're going to repossess my car? I just told myself that I'm financially independent and give away more money than I make!"

After two, three, or fifty tries at it, my brain had enough and started a full-scale rebellion. Reminding me at every turn that I was lying to myself. To make it worse, all of the fears of inadequacy and regret I carried with me came roaring in as back up.

Any time we go counter to our perceived reality and try to fake it, our conscious minds will not take it quietly. I know of a handful of people that claim success with fake-it-till-you-make-it. After more than a decade of seeing the practice ruin people's self-esteem, I can only conclude that they are exceptional. As with anything else, if it works for you, I won't try to stop you. If it doesn't, be honest with yourself and get ready to make some real progress.

Can personal and financial success exist together?

All of the people that I viewed as successful in my early professional years were workaholics. Many of them were also alcoholics or drug addicts and couldn't keep a relationship together to save their life.

I grew up in a family that emphasized love and caring for one-another, but was always broke. The magazines, then and now are packed with stories of people giving up their careers because they want to spend time with their family.

Is it impossible to be incredibly successful professionally and financially while having a strong family structure and caring relationships?

The popularized theory says you should strive to achieve balance. Make a dividing-line and give equal parts of your time and attention to your professional life and to your personal life. That sounded nice at first, but really didn't capture what a full life looked like in my mind's eye.

Why can't I have a life without lines of separation?

Who says that I must put a clock on what I do and when I do it?

Why shouldn't I be able to have it all and live in total fulfillment?

I can, and so can you.

Why do similar people get such different results?

When you study people from all walks of life, you realize that we are all completely different and still very much alike. Experiences and perceptions are the only things that we put a unique stamp on.

It's because of this phenomena that two people of identical background, education, and current circumstance can have totally different reactions to the same input.

I watched dozens of people that were very similar to me in all categories, go through the same training and end up in different places.

We would set the same goals for seemingly the same reasons, work them with equal effort, and never arrive at the same result. How is that possible?

I relate the difference to a biblical building lesson. If you give two people the exact same materials with which to build a house, except that one builds on a rock and the other builds on sand…

>   one will stand and the other will fall.

All of the gurus focused on what people do *after* getting started. I've discovered that the real issue is where people start from.

Until we get solid and secure in our starting position, our efforts will always vary and we'll never know why.

Why do I fall back after making such progress?

Fewer things are more disheartening than working your tail off to get somewhere, only to realize that you're going in circles.

More than 87% of the people I've interviewed and worked with experience the personal let down of building toward a goal and then ending up back at square-one.

Sometimes there's an obvious adversity or problem that starts the tailspin. Other times, you're clueless as to what happened, but you know that you're right back where you started.

Having this happen once is aggravating. Repeating the experience is enough to make someone give up.

Very similar to the analogy of building on sand, when we grow our lives grow beyond the capacity of our support structure, we eventually fall. The weight of our progress is too much and the pressure exposes where we are weak.

Developing that strong foundation gives us the strength to build a bigger life and sustain it for the long-term.

How do I know what I'm afraid of and make it go away?

One of the most generic diagnoses for failure or lack of success is fear. If we find ourselves unable or unwilling to get something done, we automatically assume that we must be afraid of something.

With that in mind, we focus our energy on discovering what fear has us in its grips.

Fear does not grip us. We grip fear.

Fear and darkness are similar in their roles. Both of them are nothing by themselves. Darkness is the absence of light. Without light, darkness has no reference or meaning.

Darkness cannot exist in the presence of light.

Fear is the absence of belief. When we believe in our abilities and ourselves, fear has no meaning or relevance. When we turn our efforts to understanding our belief and away from finding a fear, we notice that fears seem to disappear on their own.

Fear cannot exist in the presence of belief.

Why does my self-confidence fluctuate so much?

"One day I'm the top dog. The next, I'm the fire hydrant."

You might be able to relate to the client of mine that coined that phrase. I know I can. It's as if the stars determine my ability to make things happen and my self-confidence is as unpredictable as the weather.

When we step back and look at what is going on, we see that our confidence directly relates to our sense of direction in life.

If I'm unsure of my purpose or wavering with what I want, my ability to believe in myself drops. This runs the gambit, from life in general all the way down to a simple project.

By existing day-to-day without a clearly defined direction for my life or project, I'll be pushed around by whatever outside forces are the strongest.

When I have the fortitude that comes with a strong, conscious mindset, self-confidence is in ample supply.

I've failed before, why won't it happen again?

The biggest threat to your future is your past. In fact, the images of failure are frequently more vivid than those of success.

Because we have all of this baggage with us, our minds have an easy time of talking us out of a new or repeat adventure.

We consider a goal or possibility and begin to get excited about how our lives would change for the better if we went for it. As soon as these thoughts begin, our brain kicks into self-preservation mode and tries to save us from potential embarrassment.

"Speak in front of your entire company? You don't really think that you can do that, do you?"

"Remember in the third grade when you tried to read your story in front of the class? You messed up a word and a couple of the kids laughed. You wouldn't want that to happen again, would you?"

"Big opportunities like that are for other people, not you."

The internal dialogue is brutal. We replay the failures and misses from our past and treat ourselves as if we are still the same person that didn't make it before. We have to learn from our past and allow ourselves to move on.

Why can't I get rid of negative thoughts?

The most repetitive advice I received when introduced to personal development was to get rid of negative thoughts. All of the self-help literature referred to eliminating negative thinking as a sure fire way to have positive impact.

Unfortunately for me, I felt like a total failure when I tried to do it.

No matter how hard I worked to get rid of a negative thought, it never seemed to leave. In fact, the harder I tried to get rid of it, the stronger it seemed to become. I began to wonder if my mind was wired in a way that made it impossible.

My work environment reinforced my doubts. Any mention of negativity around the office sent people running like they were escaping an alien invasion.

The longer I contemplated the idea of eliminating negative thoughts and living in denial that negativity exists, the more idiotic it sounded. I can't remember who I heard it from, but one phrase hit me like a ton of bricks one day. What you resist persists.

By giving all of my energy to pushing negativity away, I pulled my energy from the positive things I wanted. But how could I reverse the trend? The negative things were always there. You've heard the phrase, if you can't beat them, join them. Well, if you can't get rid of them, learn to use them to get what you want.

How do I find my life's purpose?

It's the mythical quest that has lead people into the desert for centuries. What does my life mean and who is going to tell me?

Raised in the Christian faith, I read and heard numerous references to gifts, talents, and purposes that someone might have.

Even more stories surrounded people having a dramatic epiphany that revealed their God-given purpose on this earth. A *burning bush* experience.

What most of us miss, as we are waiting for the lightning bolt of clarity, is that we are infusing our daily lives with purpose.

Once we begin to recognize and tap into that lower level purpose, the grand purpose of our lives starts to take shape.

Why do I procrastinate?

Frustration reaches a critical point when we have something we want to do, there's nothing in our way, and we still don't do it. Every time you look at the task, a sick feeling in your stomach appears.

We tell ourselves that we "should" do it and might even convince ourselves that we "need" to do it… but don't.

So instead, we beat ourselves up and accept the label, procrastinator.

Similar to fear, procrastination is a generic diagnosis that has multiple causes. We could take a room of 100 people that are putting something off and drill down to find out what is actually keeping them from moving.

Once we've reached the core of their individual issue, it could be different from everyone else. In the hundreds of people I've worked with that considered themselves procrastinators, all of them had unrealized, underlying reasons for avoiding the action.

Once we brought the real reason into the light, they were able to address it directly and the bias for avoiding action disappeared. You have that same opportunity.

Pay attention for places you want to label with procrastination and make note of what we uncover. You'll see that procrastination is a symptom with many causes. Fix the causes and the symptoms go away.

Is it really possible for anyone to be successful?

While I stood at the bottom of the mountain, looking at all the people at the top, I wondered if I had what it took to get there. When I shared my concerns with others, they echoed the same thoughts.

Every time I pushed myself to climb and then slipped or fell, it became that much harder to believe I was capable.

The idea that people are born for success or have been lucky to get there is a temptation and a trap. If we give in to attributing their success to factors out of our control, we lose. We assume the victim stance and retreat to the safety of mediocrity. The one place that success isn't.

Those at the top, and on their way to the top, have come from numerous backgrounds and pedigrees. They climb with different styles and for different reasons.

What they have in common is a mindset that affords them the power and flexibility to have success on their terms. Now it is time to define your terms and get started toward your mountaintop.

Chapter 6

Time to Build Yours

Awareness

We had driven three hours to attend an early-morning meeting of our National Speakers Association regional chapter. My friend Price and I were looking for guidance on becoming professional speakers and the NSA seemed like a good place to start.

I had amassed a significant amount research and tools regarding mindset and wanted to make a living sharing that story. Price wanted to share his story too, but his was a little easier to tell.

At 18-years-old, Price was the passenger in a car crash that rendered him a quadriplegic.

Ever the indomitable spirit, he went on to become the only quad to graduate from Ohio State's law program and chased his dreams where ever they led. I was fortunate enough that those dreams brought him to the Ozarks where we met.

Though Price never required sympathy, he did require accommodations. His 300 pound wheel chair was a modern marvel, but not very useful on stairs.

So, after navigating the hotel parking garage, we found the lobby and went to the registration counter to get directions to the meeting room.

The lovely clerk at the desk made eye contact with each of us and gave a warm greeting. Price asked about the NSA meeting location and she informed us that it was downstairs in one of the conference rooms.

Without a thought, I motioned to Price's wheelchair and asked, *"What is the best way for us to get down there?"*

Looking Price directly in the eyes she asked, *"Will you be taking the stairs or the elevator?"*

As we entered the meeting room, I was still buzzing about the clerk's lack of awareness.

> *"She went through all the motions of great customer service, but I don't think she had a conscious thought go through her head. How hard is it to be aware of something as obvious as a big red wheelchair? She was so wrapped up in herself that she wasn't conscious of anything around her."*

We picked a table close to the front and as I sat down, I noticed a sharply dressed young man at the very front of the room. His chestnut brown suit and cream shirt set off his bright green tie with a subtle paisley pattern in it.

The main thing that caught my eye was the brightly colored Oakley sunglasses he was wearing... *inside!*

"Get a load of that guy," I whispered, leaning in to Price, *"How cool does he think he is?"*

Price paused thoughtfully and replied, *"I think he's blind PJ."*

Thinking that Price was setting me up for a joke, I played along. *"What on earth makes you think that?"*

"Mostly the big seeing-eye dog sitting beside him."

After a decade of research, teaching, and applying the Elements of Personal Choice, I've learned one other thing must be added to the mix.

The original members of group A had things moving and in place when I met them. Whatever had happened for each of them to form their mindset was largely unconscious.

None of them were walking around, pondering the implications of purpose, belief, forgiveness, action, gratitude, and vision. Those things were already operating properly in their mindsets, but not because they knew about them.

When I shared my findings with those I still had access to, they were even more excited.

"Now I can take it to a whole new place because I'm aware of what I'm doing!"

Awareness is the bridge that lets the rest of us get across to the land of milk and honey that group A has long enjoyed.

We can find awareness in simple scenarios, like the one in which I severely embarrassed myself by not noticing a 100-pound German Sheppard sitting beside a guy in sunglasses. There is also a greater opportunity to use awareness for achieving and growing a successful, fulfilling life.

I first began to understand awareness as a tool for personal growth in the unlikely world of manufacturing.

Good manufacturers remain aware of what is going on in their processes so they know when things are working well and when there is need for concern. Because of this, awareness is also the foundation from which all quality management systems build.

Lean, SixSigma, TQM, etc., all rely on the company and its people staying aware on a regular basis.

Initially, awareness stems from verbalizing and documenting the processes. Knowing how each piece progresses and integrates with the others is vital to a successful operation. More than 90% of all manufacturing problems exist because different departments do not realize how they influence each other.

When I've lead groups through process mapping, it is often the first time individuals see how they function within the whole. There is a new appreciation and importance for each step in their day. For the first time, they are aware and understand where they are in the scope of possible quality.

If a manufacturing process requires six steps from beginning to end, the people involved in each of those steps must understand what goes on up and downstream.

Normally we think, higher production means more money. Bigger is better. But if the people in step number four focus only on producing as much as possible, they may cause a bottleneck at step number five and a void at step number three. Through their singular focus on one part of the process, they destroy the efficiency of the whole.

Awareness brings appreciation for how everything works together so we can operate at our optimum capability.

The first level of awareness also creates a starting point. To improve, we need a baseline to measure against. Where are we now?

I've been personally involved with 14 different quality audits and read of 100's more, where a company claimed they did not make any improvements implementing new quality practices.

Each time, the audit began by asking the company for their baseline and current numbers for comparison. Not once were the baseline numbers provided.

How can we accurately say if something did or did not work if we don't know where we started? We can't. First level awareness helps us establish where things are and puts a dot on the map that says, *"I am here."* Without the clarity of establishing a baseline, there is no way to measure progress or make improvements.

The second level of awareness happens during the process. It may seem obvious that you are aware while in motion, but motion does not equal awareness. This is where the phrase, *going through the motions*, comes from. We do things without thinking or noticing what is actually happening.

In a production line environment, unaware workers can create bottlenecks and voids that threaten to shutdown everyone around them.

When they are aware of their influence up and downstream, they can observe potential pile-ups and make adjustments in process to correct for the moment. Bringing awareness to the act allows for greater insight and efficiency.

From a personal perspective, I have used this level of awareness to make course corrections and redirect my energy for best use. Since we are establishing and heightening your awareness first, you will see opportunities to make the best use of what you are learning.

Your conscious efforts, repeated, give your subconscious mind a pattern to follow. These patterns make you the person everyone else is in awe of because of how you handle life. With patterns in place, which you have intentionally designed, every situation slows down and you see ways to make things better that other people miss because it is all moving too fast for them.

Finally, quality management systems bring awareness to the evaluation stage. We planned the process and executed the process, now we look to see how we can make it better. The questions are simple, direct, and powerful.

1. What did we plan for?

2. How did we perform according to plan?

3. What did we learn while performing toward the plan?

4. How can it be better next time?

This is the cyclical nature of improvement. *Plan, execute, evaluate, improve, plan, execute....*

The greatest companies in the world use quality management systems to promote continual improvement and growth. I studied them continually while working for my MBA and have gone to numerous trainings that focus on the awareness needed for continual improvement. Companies spend millions to get these systems in place because of the potential return on investment.

Still yet, I have seldom seen any effort put toward making the same system important for the individual life.

My primary role when coaching or consulting with someone regarding mindset is to first, heighten their awareness. When properly guided, our mindsets respond like a system that determines the quality of our lives. To take control of our mindsets we must first be aware.

Awareness alone holds the key to lasting and meaningful change. We cannot intentionally influence things of which we are unaware.

At this point in the journey, we have already gained considerable awareness so consider that a head start.

You are now aware of the role your mindset plays in determining the quality of your life. You are also aware there is a way to take control of your mindset and make it give you what you have asked. These little bits of awareness are the first steps of freedom and prosperity.

As we move through the remaining six elements of personal choice, you will gain a new awareness of how life works. You will see what life really is and decide how you want to define success. There is also a bit of fun headed your way.

Mindset Moment
Maintaining awareness allows you
to systemize success.

Chapter 7

Time to Build Yours

Going from Aware to Conscious

You know that feeling of being in on a secret or a joke. Things are happening around you and the people involved do not know what you know. Some might look at things in amazement and others might not notice what is happening at all.

Your perspective is different though because you have the inside scoop. The person next to you says, *"Wow! I never saw that coming."*

You on the other hand, knew what was going on all along and have perfect clarity as to why things happened as they did.

Prepare to have that happen a lot, as you understand more about mindset and heighten your awareness toward the impact on the world. These will become your ***"Mindset Moments."***

A term that you will often see used interchangeably with awareness is consciousness. There are several spiritual connotations to the word consciousness, which we will also use, but our primary use is referring to the simple act of being aware.

The reason to get used to both words is that a conscious life is the one worth living. Only a conscious life, one full of awareness, gives us the proper perspective for shaping our lives daily.

This is important because our tendency is to think that we have to go without in order for someone else to have plenty. In short, there is scarcity.

Thinking of scarcity isn't being conscious to what is. Life is fully abundant. There is no natural scarcity imposed on us. Only those limitations we put on ourselves.

By seeking awareness, you will see that as you take care of yourself and define success on your terms, the world will expand and bring greater blessings to you and those that you love and serve.

Another benefit of living consciously is the ability to think critically. This most impressive skill allows you to see events, people, and circumstances without jumping to an instant judgment.

As a critical thinker, you can hear an angry tirade from a boss and look for the background that caused it, without jumping instantly to defense mode. You will create the chance to be the calming voice of reason instead of escalating the situation.

Critical thinkers also solve problems more effectively because they do not bog themselves down in the emotional drama associated with most conflicts.

By staying conscious of your mindset, you will find yourself detaching from the emotion of the problem so you can view it in a CAT-scan type of perspective. You will see more angles than the people around you see and easily move toward the clear solution.

If you end this book with no other skills except critical thinking, your life will be enhanced beyond financial measurement. It takes critical thought to reveal the opportunities around you, which will unleash your magnificent life.

A good friend of mine, Therese Kienast, who founded a company and methodology called Radical Leadership, introduced me to the idea of a magnificent life.

Though I am not much of a poetry buff, she shared a poem by Ralph Waldo Emerson to help me appreciate the kind of impact living a magnificent life has.

I have included the poem on the next page for you to read and reflect upon. His words really capture the essence of what you and I are doing together with this book.

What we commonly call man,

The eating, drinking, counting, planting man,

Does not as we know him represent himself,

But misrepresents himself.

Him we do not respect.

But the soul, whose organ he is,

Would he let it appear through his action,

Would make our *knees bend*.

When it breathes through his intellect, it is genius.

When it breathes through his will, it is virtue.

When it breathes through his affection, it is love.

-Ralph Waldo Emerson

Our goal with this program is to bring you awareness of your soul and teach you how to let it breathe. To grant you access to the *knee-bending life* within you.

Begin to think of yourself as Emerson did: the organ of your soul. Release your grip and let your soul breathe its magnificence through you.

Another common thing is the idea of perfection. Banish it from your mind. Nothing in this world is about perfection. No one seeks perfection and finds it.

We only find perfection when we look back.

Some of the most perfect days in my life, probably yours too, came as a result of solving a problem or conquering a challenge. It might have been a crazy, messed up day according to our plans, but became a life-long family memory.

Had we planned what would be perfect, none of those things would have entered into the equation. No one plans for problems or challenges when thinking of *"perfect."* Perspective brings perfection.

I would ask you to focus on something that is far more impressive than striving for perfection… constantly improving.

Just the idea of constant improvement makes people smile. There is more action in improving because you have to do something first. You cannot improve on something that has not been done at least once.

Isn't that how you would like people to think of you? Being willing to go for it and make something happen?

Would those looking to you for an example benefit more from you getting everything perfect the first time or messing it up, regrouping, and going again? You know the answer to that one.

And like in the quality management systems, by seeking improvement, you are constantly aware. You are aware of what you are attempting, the result, and what you can do to make it better.

A life of constant improvement is more fun, more rewarding, and more memorable than any plan for perfection.

Establishing your baseline

Awareness runs through the remainder of this program and, like all of the other elements, is intertwined in everything you do. So let's establish a baseline for our journey of improvement.

To make this work best for you, I request that you get a journal or notebook, which you dedicate to recording your answers in these exercises. You will get the most of this experience by collecting your thoughts in one place.

When you are ready, write down where you are in each area of your life. This can be as simple as a bullet list or as detailed as a full narrative on how you feel about things right now. The key is to be aware.

Write answers that mean something to you, not generic phrases like, *"doing fine," "good," or "needs improvement."* What does *"fine"* or *"good"* mean in that area.

We'll come back and get these answers for other parts of the program so take your time and make it worth it. Besides, how will you know if this program was a success if you don't know where you started?

Areas of awareness – Remember, this isn't about grading or judging yourself. We just want to establish a level of awareness so that you get maximum benefit from this point forward.

> My relationships with my children (individually)
>
> Relationship with my spouse or significant other
>
> Relationships with my parents (if your parent have passed, how do feel about your relationship at the time they died)
>
> Relationship with coworkers, employees, boss
>
> Quality and number of friendships (name your top 5 friends)
>
> What do your relationships tell you about your life right now?

Describe your level of fulfillment and satisfaction with your:

> Family

> Career

> Spirituality

> Physical fitness

> Hobbies

> Habits and routines

> Community involvement

> Life overall

What area or areas do you want growth and improvement in first?

Do you have a clear picture of your path forward in life?

Write a statement about where you are in your life and how the acknowledgement makes you feel.

Now that you've established awareness of where you're current mindset has you, let's get in to the elements that are going to bring it under your control.

Just as we discussed in the introduction, with these elements at your conscious disposal, achieving prosperity will seem as simple as flipping a switch.

S.W.I.T.C.H.

S. – See it. This is your *Vision* of the result. You have to know what success looks like or you'll never know when you arrive.

W. – Why. Your *Purpose* for wanting the result must be so strong that it guides you through any difficulty.

I. – Immunity. The ability to *Forgive* yourself and others for past wrongs and give yourself permission to make mistakes in the future.

T. – Trust. You must *Believe* in your ability to make your vision a reality.

C. – Conquer. Only through *Action* can all of the other elements achieve their full potential and reward you with your desires.

H. – Honor. The basis for having more in your life is *Gratitude* for the things you have already.

This is your S.W.I.T.C.H. The means by which you are going to take total control of your life. I have made you aware of its existence. Now you are going to learn how to reach out and turn it on.

Mindset Moment
You have a greater life waiting
inside of you. Building your mindset
will let it breathe and grow.

Chapter 8

S.W.I.T.C.H.

SEE IT! –
What is your Vision

"This isn't what I envisioned," he said.

Jeff was trying to explain why he felt so frustrated with his business growth. *"I'm here at the office or on client appointments all the time. My family is falling apart because I'm constantly working."*

*"So what **did** you envision?"* I queried. *"How did all of this look in your mind when you decided to grow your business?"*

"Just like everybody else's'," he replied without hesitation. *"I wanted a business like my mentors. I saw myself with the same business, income, and lifestyle that they have."*

"So describe what that looks like, Jeff," I requested. *"What looks different about their lives than what you've created for yourself? Pick one person that you want to emulate and describe their life as you see it."*

Over an hour later, Jeff had described the lifestyle he saw in all of the mentors and models he sought to be like. As an observer, there were a couple of things that stood out about his descriptions. All of the people that Jeff knew personally were in totally different places in their lives than he was.

Second, when he described the people he didn't know personally, but admired their businesses, he didn't mention anything about their home lives.

"Jeff, I gotta tell you straight. From my vantage point, you've created a business exactly like all of the people you described."

"I know!" He sounded so exasperated, *"But I'm not happy and I know my family isn't happy. What's the point in this business success if the rest of my life bombs?"*

At that point, we backed up and looked at each one of the people he described again. We looked at each piece of their lives that Jeff could answer first-hand. Each of the mentors that he knew personally had different home lives than Jeff.

His scenario included a stay-at-home wife, four kids between 5 and 13, and all of the activities that go with a family that size. None of his mentors was in that spot.

Over half were empty nesters and the rest ranged from single, to divorced, to never wanted kids. The parts of their lifestyles that he coveted involved a level of selfishness because they were not responsible for anyone else.

They could take off on a moment's notice for a weekend away or go to dinner whenever they felt like it. Staying at the office was easier for some because there wasn't a family at home to care for and love.

Jeff didn't build a vision of his own. He borrowed vision from others that had the life he thought that he wanted. That vision was so clear and strong that he was building the exact same thing for himself. Every decision he made brought him closer and closer to realizing the lifestyles of his mentors.

His family suffered the fallout because they were not in the vision.

When we broke down the lifestyles of those that Jeff did not know personally, he really could not speak to their family situation. He did not know if they were married, had children, or were remotely happy with anything other than their businesses.

The visions he borrowed from them didn't extend past the office. Again, the vision was so clear and strong that he was building the same lifestyle. A bigger business, but no consideration for life outside of the office.

Jeff understood the power of a vision since he was creating the exact vision he held. His previous statement about, *"This isn't at all what I envisioned,"* was simply not true.

The truth is that he didn't extend his vision to include all of the things that were making him unhappy.

Namely his family. Jeff had to make some decisions about how he wanted his life to look.

Einstein said that imagination is the preview to life's coming attractions. Knowing what we do about the results of his imagination, I think we can assume that he had a keen insight to the subject.

Fortunately, we also know that Einstein was not the first or last to recognize the benefits of picturing your desired result before attempting to accomplish it. Starting with the end in mind is all about having a vision.

Like many other elements that have a spiritual equivalent, having a vision is actually very practical. It doesn't require a sweat lodge, eating desert roots, or 20 years of meditative practice to accomplish.

Having a vision is simply creating a picture of what you want that you can feed to your subconscious.

This is important because our minds work in pictures. Test it out.

Think of the word, vision. What do you see? If you said, *"the word, vision,"* you'd be right. You created a picture of the word. Countless people I have talked to say they can't visualize. If you *saw* the word, VISION, in your head... you visualized. It really is that simple.

If you are still uncomfortable with the concept, describe to yourself or someone else, how to get to your house from your local store.

Heighten your awareness. As you describe what to do, your mind is giving you pictures of each turn, stop, and landmark. It's the same concept with visualizing a future result. You can do this.

The purpose of vision as it pertains to your mindset is a simple one. If we are working toward a life we can define as "successful," we have to know what success looks like.

Once we have a picture of success, we feed it to our subconscious. Our subconscious minds are like goal seeking machines. When we give it a picture, it seeks to align our outside circumstances with the picture we've provided.

In doing so, it sets up the filter, your mindset, to find things that make the picture, reality. Opportunities that might have slipped by come into focus. An adversity that used to throw you into a tailspin is now recognized as a chance to draw closer to your vision. That's why visualizing the desired end result, before you even begin, is so useful.

Jeff's example is a great one to share because it shows how powerful a vision can be and why the other Elements of Personal Choice must be in place with the vision. You will understand more clearly as we go along, but the bottom line is that Jeff employed vision without gratitude. He could clearly see what he wanted, but he did not honor what was great in his life while building the vision.

My job as Jeff's coach was to make him aware of what was happening, share my perspective on his situation, and give him tools to make his own decisions. Telling him what he needed to do with his life is off limits.

It is the same with you. I get the privilege of providing powerful insights, useful structure, and asking big questions so that you can make your life whatever you choose.

Jeff stayed dedicated to his vision and allowed his family to fall away. His choices kept him from gratitude and purpose and I decided to fire him as a client.

Eventually, he built a roaring business that embodied everything he had hoped for... and lost it. Learn from Jeff's mistake. Embrace the power of your vision and everything we cover here, but make sure that you include all of the other elements for real success.

Now a few ground rules about visualization. You must be as self-centered and selfish as possible. That might sound a little contradictory after Jeff's story, but remember his resistance to the other elements.

If you are thinking, *"Oh but PJ, I live my life for others,"* you had better get clear about the implications.

If you really want to live a life for others, the first person that has to be cared for is you. Why do you think they have you put on the oxygen mask first on a plane before assisting anyone else?

If you're gasping for air and passed out, who's going to help the people traveling with you?

I'm not saying to think only of yourself. I'm saying to build the vision around you and your ideal life. There is a good chance that your ideal life involves significant time with those you love and providing amazing experiences for them. How are you going to do that if you don't have any clue what those experiences look like?

The strength of designing your mindset is to move with intention toward a desire. Remembering that our subconscious mind wants to align the internal picture with our external reality, we have to give it as many details as possible.

Clarity is next to Godliness. Attachment is the work of the devil.

The more clearly defined your picture, the greater your chances of accomplishing the result, but there is one caveat with the details of your vision. Be flexible.

We'll talk more about this as we go, but we cannot be so hung-up on a detail that we squash the entire vision.

One of my clients several years ago, Meredith, crafted a vision of her family living in a certain neighborhood. This neighborhood was safe, close to the best schools in the area, and represented significant accomplishment to her.

Reinforcing her desire to be there, Meredith noticed that no one ever moved out of the neighborhood. She drove through at least once a week on her way home from work, looking for realtor signs. After three months of zero availability, a sign appeared.

She got a viewing appointment, toured the house, and loved it. They made an offer right away and got word that they were number three of eight. The sellers played the supply and demand card perfectly and a bidding war ensued.

Meredith clarified her vision further by adding that particular house. She envisioned getting the kids ready for school and family parties. The way she described each detail showed me how well she understood the process. If I had not been so inexperienced at the time, I might have seen what was coming.

Two weeks after their bid, the sellers decided to pull the house off the market and stay. A health concern caused them to rethink their plans and they told the bidders to stay in touch.

Much to my surprise and joy, Meredith was amazing. Now with that part of her vision so clear, she kept right on making things happen in the rest of her life. She made good decisions and progress around the professional side of her vision and seemed very locked in. *Too locked in.*

One of her co-workers lived in the neighborhood of Meredith's vision. Two houses down from the one she was competing for.

His wife, a pediatrician, had taken a position at a specialty clinic over 140 miles away. They needed to move and wanted it to happen quickly.

He knew about the ordeal Meredith had just been through with the other house and asked her if she would consider buying their house. It was virtually identical to the other house and would save them time, hassle, and money if they could do a private deal. He would even sell it for a little under fair market value to move things along.

As Meredith relayed this surreal occurrence during our weekly call, I wanted jump. I was so happy that her dedication was paying off. Then she knocked the wind out of me.

"I told him that it sounded like a great deal, but that we're going to wait for the other house to come back on the market."

Unable to disguise my shock, *"You're going to do what?"*

"Wait for the house in my vision," she replied with a tinge of aggravation. *"It's what I've wanted this entire time."*

"If that's really the case," I replied, *"good for you. But I thought there was a different reason for wanting to be in that neighborhood that was much bigger than a specific house."*

We each grabbed our copy of Meredith's original vision statement. I had learned enough at that point to know about having a strong purpose for wanting to realize your vision. So, I had everyone I worked with write that purpose, their *"why"* along with the vision.

Meredith read the purpose for wanting to be in that neighborhood as a bullet list.

- Safety and peace of mind

- Opportunities for the kids through the schools

- More time at home because it is closer to work

- Feeling of accomplishment from fulfilling a childhood dream

Nothing about a house or even a specific street.

After a brief, but thoughtful pause, Meredith asked if we could cut our call short so she could make a different phone call.

She had gotten so attached to her vision, *to the exact house*, she almost missed an opportunity to buy the house two doors down. Her intention was around the neighborhood, but she worked a house into the vision. Not a problem, unless you get so attached to the vision that you defer an opportunity to realize your dream.

Be careful of obsessing over the vision. We'll talk more about this in the Conquer phase.

Current reality need not apply

Finally, while crafting your vision, suspend your current reality.

Forget about bills, promotions, education, current relationships, etc. This is your ideal life we are talking about. If you spend all of your time handicapping your vision with your current limitations, you will end up with what you have now.

We are visualizing what we want, not what we have. So stay in the moment, define where you want to be, and be ready to recognize and respond as your world shifts.

Let's pull together some pieces for you to build your vision with. Since we are seeking to have and be things that are different than what we currently have, I'm going to make a bold assumption: there are parts of your life that you're not happy with.

I know, it's like I'm *psychic* or something.

Because there are things we don't like, that's where I want to start... with the negatives. It's a little different approach than most of my colleagues that share the "motivational" label, but I find it very useful.

What I don't want

Begin by listing the things in your life that you aren't happy with. Go back to your baseline list and use it as a guide to identify areas of your life that contain places you want to improve. Be as specific as you can.

What I do want

Now take your list from *What I don't want* and turn the negative statements to intentions. i.e. "I don't like the way I feel or look in a bathing suit." Turn it around to, "I want to look and feel good in a bathing suit." Simple, right? Remember to be specific.

Paper dolls

At this point we have some guidance for our vision, but it is still incomplete. The idea of creating your vision is adding life and clarity to your desires. If you're anything like me, you'll constantly add and change details of your vision as you go along. I'm always evaluating and finding things that I like better than others. A new beach or favorite restaurant. This is a living thing and you can allow it to grow and flourish.

Here are a few starter questions to answer to provide the initial boost of clarity. Have fun with this and play make believe. I call it Paper Dolls because you can dress yourself up as many ways as you like. Try things on. If you don't like it or find something that suits you better, change it. Let yourself go.

Where do you live (What area, region, or country? On a beach, in the mountains, or in a major metro? You choose…this is your ideal life.)

What do you do professionally (If you could do anything you wanted…)

What is your professional environment (Paint the walls and hang the art.)

Describe your relationships with your family

How do you dress

Is your body different

Who are you friends

What are your hobbies

What are your daily routines

Are you active in your community

Have you won awards

How do you experience growth (What areas keep you growing and how?)

Travel

Formal education

Seminars

Competition

Teaching

Religion

Spirituality

How do others describe you (You get to put the words in their mouths. When people talk about you, what do they say?)

Ideal day-normal with no limitations

One of my mentors, Rich Schefren, added a detail to this exercise that helped me get over a *"reality"* barrier. His instructions were to create an ideal, normal day. A day that I would experience repeatedly. So no visits with the President or Prime Minister, unless that is part of your normal day. Fill this vision with things you want all of the time.

Now take all of the things you listed above and craft your day. Remember that this is a typical day, with as many of the things you want, and as few of the things that you don't want. We're also going to break the day into four equal sections. Concentrate on one at a time and paint a radically vivid picture. Take the lid off your thinking and go for it with no limitations.

> What time does your day start? Where are you for the first 4 hours? Whom do you spend it with and what are you doing?

> Where are you for the second 4 hours of your day? What do you do and with whom?

> How do you spend the third 4 hours of your day? Where does it take you and whom do you see?

> For the fourth and final 4 hours of your day, who is around? Where are you and what activity fills these last wonderful hours?

Never asked how much you make

Something you may have noticed; I never asked you to record how much money you make in your ideal, perfect day. There is an important reason for that and now is as good of a time as any to cover it. Money doesn't matter.

Now relax… I don't mean that you won't need money to make all of this stuff happen. Money doesn't matter because it is not the end, it is only a means to the end. Our goal is to identify your ideal, normal day. It really doesn't matter how much money it requires to have that day. Our only concern is what it looks like.

Money is the biggest limitation people put on their visions. And since I don't have a stick long enough to poke you when you let your current limitations sneak in… you'll have to police yourself on this one. Rest assured, money will find its way back in to all of this, but only when it matters and in its proper place.

When people set income goals under traditional goal-setting models, they usually go at it all wrong. I was taught to determine how much I wanted to make and map it back to the activity necessary to get it. The vision was for the things the money would buy. That approach puts money as the goal and the lifestyle as the motivation. Totally wrong.

To harness the real power of the exercise, we don't look at money… we look at what the money will provide. We'll talk more about this in Purpose.

Once we've established what we want, and brought the rest of the Elements of Personal Choice into alignment, the money shows up only as a way of getting there. Similar to picking a vacation destination *and then* looking for the best route to get there. Money isn't the destination, only a route of travel.

Remember that as we go along.

Chapter 9

S.**W**.I.T.C.H.

WHY? -
Defining your Purpose

If you have a child past the age of three, you know the power of the word, "why."

Maybe it's because of the way people burn out and respond to us as children that causes us to stop asking *"why."* It seems that somewhere between childhood and adolescence we start to accept things on face value and stop digging to understand why things are the way we see them. This lack of probing is at the root of why 98% of the population lives without clear direction in their lives.

The clearest example is from the school of goal setting. When I first learned of personal development and self-improvement, the company I worked for gave me an audio course on setting goals. I dug into the material and began understanding the value of defining a goal, mapping out a plan for accomplishment, and getting into action.

The problem I encountered wasn't really covered by the material though. I started out fine... lots of enthusiasm and excitement, but before long I felt deflated… stalled out.

I went to my supervisor and asked him what was wrong. His well-meaning response was to show me examples of other people in the company and the goals that they set for themselves. So I took a look and talked to some them about their goals. Wow. They had some huge goals and I began to think that mine were simply not big enough to keep me motivated.

Now armed with much bigger goals than I had before, I took off after my fortune. And just like before, I stalled. My momentum came to a standstill and all pursuit of the goals stopped.

"I must not be cut out for the great things that those goals would provide me."

You can imagine how disappointed I was. You might have experienced the feelings yourself. Why couldn't I maintain my desire and movement toward the goals? What I have learned since then is so fundamental to reaching goals, any goals, that you might miss it on the first pass.

There were two reasons for my inability to make my goals reality. I lacked purpose and belief. We'll cover belief later in the program. For now, I want to talk about purpose.

Remember the 3 year-olds question? *"Why?"* That's what I was missing. I have come to find out; it's what most people are missing when it comes to setting goals. We set amazing, grand, and important sounding goals and have no idea of the reason behind the goal. Why does it matter to us and why would we pursue it anyway?

In my case, I looked at the goals of others as the model for setting my own. They set production goals, so I set production goals. They set income goals, so I set income goals. The pattern went on and on with one common result. I didn't reach the goals.

I understood what it took to get there intellectually. Mapping out goals is easy with a little instruction. The steps were obvious and attainable, but the drive to make them happen disappeared right after I got started.

If you get what I am about to share with you, the world is yours and you will achieve every goal you ever set.

Before declaring a goal for yourself, you must have a purpose for achieving it that is deep enough to drive you to completion. Without a purpose (your why) that has enough power to offset the difficulty of the goal, you will always fail. As long as you set goals with powerful purpose, you will always reach them.

This applies way beyond goal setting too. Think of any area of your life that presents challenges for you and is typically difficult for you to get through. I'll use... a family gathering as an example.

November and December are months that personal coaches really earn their money because of the baggage that the holidays bring. People dread the same old tired routines that play every year. The judgmental aunt, gossiping cousin, and bratty kids are as common as turkey at Thanksgiving. For years, I listened to people lament the inevitable result of the gathering and then ask themselves, *"Why do I even go to these things?"*

Finally, I made someone answer the question. It wasn't my best move as a coach, but my client Karen happened to ask herself that question on a day that I felt a little irritable... *"Yeah,"* I asked, *"why do you go?"*

The stunned silence was almost comical. *"Um. What do you mean, 'why'?"*

"If it is so miserable, why do you continue to go?"

"Because it's family and I have to go."

"First of all, no you don't. You choose to go. Secondly, why do go? What do you hope to get out of it?"

The answer to that question is where our lesson really begins.

Regardless of how you would answer that question, the underlying result is always the same. When we have a purpose going into an endeavor, our chances of receiving a sense of fulfillment from the endeavor increase dramatically. Without a purpose, we give up all power to influence the outcome.

I'll help you dig deep for purpose in a bit, but let's say that your answer to the question above was something like Karen's, *"I go because having our family together is important to my mom and like to do my part to make her happy."*

In that case, your purpose for going is to; focus your energy on your mom and doing what you can to make her happy. Imagine how much easier it would be to enjoy yourself if that was the only thing you needed accomplish? You control the outcome because it is all within your being.

> You're doing **your** part. (not fretting over your lazy uncle)

> **You're focusing** on your mom. (not your sister's monstrous children)

> You're purpose is **centered in love**. You are letting your *soul breathe.*

All the other junk falls away when purpose guides your actions. The attitudes of others are their responsibility, not yours. Your entire time there is spent fulfilling what you intend to get out of it. As a result, you enhance everyone else's experience by default.

Something to pay attention to in this example is how you gauge success. Your purpose is to *do your part* to make your mom happy. Not to *make your mom happy*. Her emotional state is not your responsibility and to make it your goal is a set up for failure. Be satisfied to do your part and allow the rest to happen as it will. Be clear about your purpose.

Karen's clearly defined purpose for attending her family function did more than make it tolerable.

> *"More than one of my siblings commented that this was the best time they remembered since we were kids. I didn't say a word, except to agree. There is no doubt that my attitude had an impact on everyone else though. After the first couple of things happened that would normally send me over the edge, I just let them go and stuck to my purpose. Everyone else seemed to follow suit."*

How can something as simple as purpose make that big of a difference? The same way something as simple as a compass can guide sailors across an ocean. It provides an internal guide that stays true no matter what is happening on the outside.

If a storm covers the stars and brings 50-foot waves up to block your view, grab the wheel and steer by the compass.

When the storm subsides, and it always does, you're still on course and farther along. In the meantime, all of those that set out without a compass crash against rocks or are scrambling in a panic to figure out where they are. Purpose makes a difference by giving you:

Perspective – Things in your life fall into their proper positions relative to your purpose

Context – Purpose helps determine, specify, and clarify the meaning of an event

Motivation – When the purpose is big enough, taking action is second nature

Flexibility – Fulfilling purpose happens in the moment, so we are always ready to make adjustments

Attraction – Purpose is sexy. It draws people to you that help to fulfill your aim

Engagement – Focus is an automatic bi-product of purpose

Creativity – Purpose removes anxiety and encourages a playful spirit

Commitment – Temptation to waiver is gone because of the confidence that purpose brings

Guidance – Combined with your Vision, Purpose funnels you toward fulfillment

Clarity - Decisions fall away as Purpose makes the way forward obvious

Purpose plays an even more important role in your life when you consider the number of people that look to you for an example. Allowing purpose into your everyday interactions elevates you in society. People with purpose stand out.

You become the person that seeks and identifies purpose for your:

> Family
>
> Business
>
> Civic organizations
>
> Churches
>
> Social groups

As you move with purpose, others learn to do the same.

Remember that purpose is more functional than just, *"your life's purpose."* What is most fun about gaining awareness of the role purpose plays is that you will begin to see patterns. By defining purpose for everything you do and seek, from the smallest to the largest of events, you'll recognize a central theme through all of them.

This theme is different from most of us but it doesn't have to be. The idea is to see your life's purpose reflected in the minor purposes. I bring this up because you don't have to tackle your life's purpose first. You'll eventually want to get there, but it isn't required on your first go.

One other thing. Purpose is different from goals or strategy. Where goals and strategy are carried out and accomplished, purpose is ongoing. Instead of accomplishing your purpose, you fulfill it. Purpose transcends goals and can carry you from one goal to another. Watch for that distinction.

Now we're going to define your purpose. Notice I said define, not discover. People waste their entire lives waiting for God to hit them with a lightning bolt and reveal their purpose to them. It doesn't work that way.

As an adult, I spent years wandering around my own personal desert looking and waiting for that burning bush. Secretly hoping that my purpose would have certain things involved. Stuff that I really liked and would be happy to spend my life doing. However, my upbringing suggested that a person's purpose might not always be something they enjoyed. *"You can't run from your calling."* I saw many other people subscribing to that same notion.

It's a load of crap.

Regardless of your religious beliefs or disbeliefs, we are not puppets on a string. We are freethinking beings that are at choice for everything we experience. Every minute that we spend waiting for someone or something else to tell us, why we are here, is a wasted minute. Asking for guidance to sort things out is fine. But when the dust settles, *we* decide our purpose. We choose our destination and set our course.

You've been given and have developed certain gifts and talents throughout your life. Those talents and gifts should have something to do with your purpose, but they can manifest as your purpose in many different forms. While considering your purpose, let your soul breath.

Use your Vision statement to recognize important pieces toward your purpose. Knowing how your vision looks, use the picture to define your purpose. When people look back at your life and say, *"she/he was about _____,"* what do you want them to say? That's where we'll start.

Descriptive statement – When people celebrate your life, what will they say? *"She/he lived her/his purpose every day and that purpose was to _____."* Once again, put the words in their mouths. What do you want them to say?

5 deep – Now that you've determined what you want them to say, let's find out why you want them to say it.

Take the answer you wrote for the previous statement and rewrite it as an affirmative statement. If you wrote, *"enrich the lives of those around her,"* in the blank above, write, *"My purpose is to enrich the lives of those around me."*

With that written, ask yourself a question. *"Why is it important to me to enrich the lives of those around me,"* or whatever it is for you. Write that answer. You're going to repeat this a total of five times. Each new answer will reveal a deeper, more meaningful layer of your purpose.

Go deep with this and really make the answers mean something.

My purpose is to

_____.

Why is that important to me? Answer.

Why is that important to me? Deeper Answer.

Why is that important to me? Even Deeper Answer.

Why is that important to me? Still Digging Answer.

Why is that important to me? Deepest Answer.

Now that you've reached your fifth answer, your understanding of what is really important to you is more clear and rich than before. Use the final answer to modify your original descriptive statement if you like. Make it yours.

With this deeper understanding, let's magnify your purpose by considering its impact.

The loss – What would the world, your community, your family, and your children lose if you failed to fulfill your purpose?

If you doubt for a moment that your purpose can have a dramatic impact... consider how important your example is to your children. Deciding to ignore your purpose is the same as staring your child in the eyes and telling them, *"You don't matter to me."*

My bet is that you would never do that. Your being is infused with too much greatness to allow it. Your purpose matters. *You matter.*

The statement – Now we fill in the blanks. Take the segments you've completed and drop the appropriate pieces into this simple framework to get started.

The first blank is your affirmative purpose from the descriptive statement and the 5 Deep exercise. Pull the purpose from there.

The second blank is from the loss exercise. Take the loss and flip it to a gain. If the world would lose a source of enrichment and possibility, the gain is, so the world has a source of enrichment and possibility.

The final product is your purpose statement. Don't worry about it being perfect to start with. Just get it written.

Once committed to paper you can tweak and craft as much as you want. Make sure to check any modifications against your soul-meter. If you make a change, read it; and if it doesn't stir your soul, scrap the change.

My purpose in life is to _____ so that _____.

This is important work. This is also where we take a serious break from traditional self-improvement courses. What we have covered so far in vision and purpose are where most of them trail off. They're done.

We know this is only the beginning. In the high-reward game of life-long success, having a vision and purpose is only the price of admission.

From here on out you will get the real difference makers that have slid under the radar until now.

> *Mindset Moment*
> *You must have a purpose for going forward or the slightest breeze will knock you back.*

Chapter 10

S.W.**I.**T.C.H.

IMMUNITY –
The Gift of Forgiveness

Kim struggled with a promotion at work for more than three weeks. The issue wasn't getting the promotion because *she had already received it!*

She was passed her over four different times for promotions before we started working together. As her performance coach, I couldn't have been happier with her success. But over the last couple of weeks there was a distinct difference in the way she was acting.

Initially, Kim would jump at every activity I gave her and answer questions honestly and with great introspection. Since the promotion though, she had struggled with performing at her best.

Thinking it was just a little bit of let down from such an emotional triumph, I gave her a little space for a week. Soon it was obvious that there was something more going on.

"Are you regretting the promotion?" I asked.

"No! Not at all. This is one of the greatest things that has ever happened to me," she replied. *"It just seems like no matter how hard I work...I just keep hearing what my dad would tell me each time I got passed over before."*

"Maybe you're just not cut out for management."

"Now I'm here and...and...I just can't get it out of my head!"

Kim's dad had died eight months earlier, and after a few minutes of empathy and pointed questions, we realized that she was still harboring resentment toward her dad because of his words. He never saw her promoted, never acknowledged that she was *"cut out for management,"* therefore she had never forgiven him.

At this point, I was in totally new ground as a coach.

All I could think to ask was, *"What would it feel like if you could let all of that go?"*

Over the course of the next few days, Kim was able to let it go. She was able to forgive her father by realizing the stranglehold all of her resentment had on her life. Once she realized that *she* could make the decision to let it all go, it was the like the clouds parted.

Not only did she shrug-off a major weight holding her back by forgiving, she granted herself immunity going forward. Making the deal with herself to go for it with full understanding that she might fail occasionally. When she failed, it didn't shut her down or hinder her movement.

Her performance improved immediately and she eventually moved from that mid-level management position to a top candidate to replace the CEO at retirement.

Since that experience with Kim, I have had several years to see this same issue with forgiveness in many other people, including myself.

In a nationwide Gallup Poll, 94% of Americans said that it was important to forgive. The same poll revealed that only 48% usually tried to forgive others. What gives?

Is it that people view forgiveness as weakness, as Friedrich Nietzsche did? Maybe we think that forgiveness is beyond us and only reserved for those with saintly qualities. Research shows that the opposite is true.

We humans are not the only ones able to display forgiveness or reconciliation. Primates show the same attributes, suggesting that forgiveness behavior is as old as life itself.

Further research by the University of Wisconsin tells us that forgiveness is not only within the reach of everyone, but is teachable with positive results.

The scientific community has engaged along with the sociological community to study and embrace this often-misunderstood concept. They have found that:

- Letting go of anger and resentment can reduce the severity of heart disease.

- In some cases, forgiving prolonged the lives of cancer patients.

- Releasing the desire for revenge (the opposite of forgiveness) can play a key role in reducing crime.

- Forgiveness is a successful tool for reconciling couples when all else has failed.

- Healing and growth accelerates in war-torn countries like Northern Ireland, South Africa, and Rwanda when a specific focus on forgiveness is used.

New studies shed light on the nature of forgiveness and certain group profiles.

- At-risk adolescents

- War veterans with post-traumatic stress and similar disorders

- Substance abusers

- The terminally ill

- Elderly patients dealing with end-of-life issues

- Domestic violence victims

- Those living with HIV/AIDS

- Physically disabled persons

- Family and friends of suicide victims

All of these studies and findings surround some high-level applications of the power of forgiveness... so what does that have to do with your success? *A lot.*

If we look at the Elements of Personal Choice like the components of a car, the effects of a forgiveness issue are easier to understand.

When we hold on to instances that cause bitterness or guilt, we are pulling on the emergency brake and jamming a foot into the brake pedal. How far can you go, how fast will you move if you are trying to drive in that state?

What is worse... if you really rev-up the engine, thinking that you are giving it your all to get somewhere, but your brakes are holding you back... what happens? You burn out. Everything fails, or at best, horribly underperforms.

Forgiveness as a tool actually works differently than the rest. Whereas all of the others *add* something to equation, forgiveness *removes* something. If we consider purpose as the engine powering the car, we can view forgiveness as releasing the brakes. If purpose is the sail on the ship, forgiveness is pulling up the anchor.

Everything gets easier with the obstacles and hindrances removed. The same effort that achieved mediocre results before, now takes you further than you imagined.

Resentment

So how do we recognize a forgiveness issue? Let's start with how the need to forgive shows up. We can classify most, if not all of the issues as either resentment or guilt.

Resentment is the easiest to associate with forgiveness because it bares the marks that we're used to. Lack of trust, feelings of anger, judgment, a want to attack, victimization, and more are the fruits of resentment. Are you feeling a knot in your stomach when you read some of these words?

Guilt

Guilt is associated more with wanting to be forgiven than in giving forgiveness. However, it is just as big of a deal for our purposes here.

Guilt manifests as many ways as resentment. Self-worth and self-esteem suffer, positive expectations for ourselves diminish, we tend to be defensive or completely disengage to avoid talking about certain subjects.

Neither guilt nor resentment carries any power. In fact, they suck you dry. They suffocate your soul and reduce your effectiveness to the point of neutrality. The biggest falsehood centers on withholding forgiveness from someone else. The lie goes,

"If I don't forgive them, I hold power over them."

LIE, LIE, LIE! The truth is the exact opposite. By holding resentment or anger, we give the object of our angst all of the power over us. There is nothing enlightened about holding a grudge. In addition, just think about the implications of how we describe this act...

Holding a grudge.

Withholding forgiveness.

Holding something *over their head.*

Where is all of the work? Who expends all of the energy? *We* are either using our power to *hold over* or *hold back.* Can you see now that a lack of forgiveness is damaging? If so, I want to make two more distinctions.

The first is that forgiveness only takes one. When you realize that you need to forgive, the other person does not have to be involved. They do not even need to realize their need to be forgiven. This is all about you.

If the other person asks for your forgiveness, you can give it and everyone has closure. If you recognize a resentment and the offender does not, big deal. Forgiveness is an inside job. Get your heart and your soul clear of the obstacle and move on.

Conversely, when we want forgiveness, it is natural to want the other person to express their forgiveness to us. If that happens, great. If not, you cannot put your world on hold while the other person gets it together. You can and must forgive yourself. More on this in a moment, but the fact is... you do not need another person to experience forgiveness.

The second distinction flies directly in the face of what I just said... *kind of.* There are only two types of people that we can offer forgiveness. Others and ourselves.

In offering forgiveness to others, number one still holds true. They do not have to be involved for us to forgive and move on. When we offer to ourselves though, we have to go a little schizophrenic and get the other party engaged in the process.

This most often occurs with our own failures from the past that don't involve anyone else. Where we set a goal and fail. Perhaps we engage in something slightly shady to get ahead. Whatever it is, the voice in your head brings it up every chance it gets. This needs forgiveness.

As I mentioned earlier, this can stem from a direct act or inaction toward someone else too. When we realize that we want forgiveness, we can ask for it from the other person.

Something that I personally missed for years in this area is that just because someone else forgives us doesn't mean that the issue is over. Regardless of the actions of the other, we still have to forgive ourselves.

So how do we discover if a forgiveness issue has our foot on the brake? There may be one or more that are obvious to you now, through your heightened awareness. Some of them might be a little fuzzy though. Maybe they are there, maybe not.

The best way to start is to consider an area that you feel stuck in. When you've gone through the exercises of vision and purpose and still find that you're unable to move forward, you need to look for resentment or guilt.

More specifically, when you consider the place you are stuck, is there an instance from the past or person that comes to mind?

Write down an area where you feel stuck. Have you reached this place multiple times? Describe the area with as much detail and emotion as you can.

Ask yourself, *"Why am I stuck here?"* Let things bubble up without forcing them to the surface. Write each one down and resist the urge to judge or edit.

Once you have exhausted the potential answers, begin at the top of the list and look for patterns and obvious obstacles. Is there a particular person or personal event that surfaces when you think of the reasons for your *stuckness*? Do you see something that needs forgiveness?

If there are no standout issues that need forgiveness, ask yourself a few more questions about each item you recorded.

"Why would this particular item be in my way or holding me back from accomplishing my goal?"

"Have I attempted a goal like this before?" If so, *"What was the outcome then?"*

Write and explore your answers.

Our first interest, once we have found an issue needing forgiveness, is to let it go. We must forgive and let the issue leave.

Believe it or not, resentment and guilt don't want to stay with us. It is our insistence that they remain that keeps them around. That is the reason behind all of the verbiage around forgiveness. They all indicate release.

The simplest way to release resentment or guilt is to just… let it go. Too simple, right?

You'll notice that the awareness of an issue makes it much more manageable. Resentment and guilt growl and intimidate you while allowed to stay in the dark.

But when we identify them and put light in their corner... we realize that they aren't scary at all.

Truthfully, they are sad and pathetic. Moreover, we see they have stayed only because we have chained them down. They growl because they are powerless and have no other means of influencing us. All they want is to leave. So let them.

Release meditation

Taking the time to sit quietly and visualize this process helps tremendously.

> Picture the dark corner and hear the growling. It is the forgiveness issue you identified earlier and it realizes it is exposed.

> Reach out beside you and find the light switch on the wall. Flip on the light and behold you aggressor... small, ugly, toothless, and more scared than you are. You actually feel sympathy for this retched creature.

> While observing the corner, now well lit and without shadow, you see the huge chains holding the creature in place. There is a lock holding the chains in place. You look from the lock, back to the creature and notice that it is still growling from fear, but staring intently at your neck.

Instinctively you reach for your neck and feel a necklace chain holding a pendant... a key. The creature knows as well as you do the key can set it free. You know what to do now.

You take the key from around your neck, walk to the lock, and release the chains. As the chains hit the floor, you expect a thud or clang, but instead... they turn to powder and blow away. The same breeze caresses you and freshens your senses. You look back to the corner just in time to see the creature walking away. It looks back at you with a look of thanks in its eyes and disappears from view.

Instead of feeling the absence of the creature, you feel the rush and exhilaration of power surging through your body. Gratitude overwhelms every sense and you smile from ear-to-ear knowing you are in control of your own life. Enjoy this moment and lock in the sensations it causes throughout your body.

As you become more comfortable with identifying issues and letting them go, you will find that a simple approach is often the best.

Be aware that you may need to repeat the process for a full release. If you have held on to something for 25 years, you might need a little more time to get over it. Also be aware, you can get over anything instantly... if you choose.

That is what all of this comes back to, choice. Speaking of choices...

There are other methods of releasing the resentment and guilt. Some of them are rather involved methods and some are simple, personal meditations like the one we just went through. Find what resonates best with you. Again, choice is the key. Do not expect a method or process to do it for you. Ultimately, you have to let it go.

Two resources are The Sedona Method and Ho'oponopono.

The Sedona Method takes you through a process of awareness and then a series of questions to achieve release. Originally created by Lester Levenson, it is now ran by Levenson's long-time protégé, Hale Dwoskin.

Ho'oponopono is an ancient Hawaiian practice of forgiveness and reconciliation. Through the use of awareness and a four phrase meditation, ho'oponopono resonates deepest with those that have experienced a real need for self-forgiveness. Like me.

The four phrases capture the elements of acknowledgment, remorse, and unconditional love. They are:

> ➢ I love you

> ➢ I'm sorry

> ➤ Please forgive me

> ➤ Thank you

You can use them in any order that suites you. The one above is my preference. If you hold the feeling of the forgiveness issue in your mind while sincerely reciting those phrases, you will begin to feel differently about it.

My go-to resource for forgiveness is prayer. Regardless of methods or process, for me, I have to know I'm right with the God of the universe in order to move forward. When that relationship is right, the rest is much easier.

This may be a very easy thing for you to do. Forgiveness is not always a stumbling-block. If it is, find the method of forgiveness that is most comfortable with you and make it happen. You will never know how powerful you can be until you do.

Mindset Moment
You cannot embrace your present
if your hands are full of the past.

Chapter 11

S.W.I.**T**.C.H.

TRUST –
The Power of Belief

"I've never done anything that big," he said.

"So what does that matter," I asked. *"There are lots of big things you had never done until you made it a goal and went for it."*

"True, but this one is somehow, different. Every time I look at it...I'm afraid."

Billy and I had worked together for two years and his record of accomplishments was impressive. At the age of 32, he had already built and sold three companies in the radiology industry for the nifty sum of $31,000,000. His fourth company, where I met him, was poised to acquire his two largest competitors and make him the big fish in a very profitable pond.

Just like every other major accomplishment under his belt, Billy had taken the goal and plugged it into a common goal setting system. He knew what individual steps were needed and in what order.

Through our work together, he knew why he wanted to accomplish the goal and had a crystal clear vision of the deal completed.

There was a problem with the deal though. Billy had repeatedly failed to perform a few simple tasks from his list during the last three months and the two competitors were threatening to join forces if he did not make the move.

Billy's goal setting and achieving system was letting him down and he didn't know why.

How about you? Have you ever set a goal that makes your heart jump? Emotionally, you want the result. Intellectually, you know that it is possible. You have a strong reason for going after it and you know what it will look like when you are there.

You have mapped the path and the only thing between you and the end of the rainbow is taking the steps to get there. Instead of taking the steps and following the yellow brick road, you freeze.

In your mind and on paper, there is no reasonable explanation for your inability to get things done. All you know is that you are not any closer to realizing the goal than you were before. What gives? Welcome to Billy's problem.

In the course of working with more than 2,500 entrepreneurs and executives, as well as struggling with this dilemma myself, I have found the common obstacle in this situation is belief. More specifically, we try to operate beyond our level of belief.

By definition, belief is something that we hold as true even though we have not experienced it through one of our physical senses. It is beyond our personal experience.

We can make assumptions based on the experiences of others, and what we can deduce through observation, but the actual experience is beyond our scope.

Visualize it this way. Reach your hand out in front of you as far as you can. Extend your fingertips, and then close your hand. Within your hand is your experience. At the end of your fingertips is belief. You might be able to touch it, but you cannot yet grasp it.

If you make $64,999 one year and set a goal to make $65,000 the next, the $64,999 is in your grasp and the $65,000 is at your fingertips. If you have never made $65,000 then you have to believe you can do it. Make sense?

In Billy's case, he had acquired, grown, and sold companies, but he had never acquired and merged two companies. Similar, yes, but not within his grasp. He had to believe that he was capable because he had never done it before.

As it turns out, he did not believe it. With all of his focus on the end goal, the goal he did not believe he could achieve, he froze. None of the other steps mattered because his focus was too far out.

The steps I took with Billy are the same that I have taken with countless others and you can use them too.

When you find yourself staring at a goal, unable to move forward, consider your level of belief. Do you really believe that you can accomplish the goal? Check in with your body when asking the question. You will experience a physical sensation that gives you the answer.

- Maybe your stomach feels sick.

- Perhaps you get a little foggy and can't think straight.

- You might feel a slight tinge of panic.

Whatever it is for you, acknowledge the signs your body gives you. When you ask yourself, *"do I believe that I can _____ ?"* do not lie to yourself.

If you cannot reply with a confident, honest, and resounding, *"YES I CAN,"* you need to do some work.

I have had plenty of times that I could not answer, *"YES."* Billy couldn't either. He had tried to convince himself of it, but only dug a deeper hole each time. So we used the tools he was familiar with to explore what was possible.

He got out his list of action steps that were necessary to reach the goal. After agreeing that these were the steps between where he was and where he wanted to be, we tackled his level of belief.

Starting with the first step outside of his experience, the one that required a little belief, he asked himself, *"Do I believe I can do this?"* His answer was a confident and honest, *"YES I CAN,"* so we moved to the next one.

"Do I believe I can do this?" Confidently and honestly, *"YES I CAN."*

We continued this exercise until he reached the step that gave him pause. Even over the phone, I could feel his entire physiology change. He tried to give a confident yes, but it felt hollow.

"You sure about that one," I asked.

He stayed silent for a moment and then said, *"I ought to be able to do this. It's stupid that I'm stuck on something so simple!"*

We took a collective deep breath and looked at his list. The sticking point was only halfway to the top. With a little reluctance, Billy agreed to take a step back and look at the last action item he honestly believed in.

I asked him, *"What would happen if we forgot about everything after this item and just worked on getting this far?"*

"I'd only be halfway to my goal!" he replied, laying on the sarcasm.

With a little heavier sarcasm I asked, *"Is that further along than you are now?"*

The answer was obvious and our experiment was set. Billy made a new goal sheet that ended with the last action step he believed in and put the other sheet in a file. Then, remarkably, he got to work.

All of the action steps on the believable goal sheet were on the original, but he had not accomplished any of them in the prior three months. In total, the shorter list's schedule was seven weeks to completion. I checked in with Billy every week to measure his progress and celebrate completed steps.

Four weeks into his seven-week list, Billy realized that he was almost done. *"I've only got two more things on this list,"* he remarked, *"what now?"*

Not really sure if this was the right thing to do, I suggested he take out the original list. *"Let's go through it from the beginning and cross off everything you've done so far."*

We took one step at a time. He told me a story about each step as we went. Some of them provided challenges he hadn't anticipated and some were much easier. A few of them disappeared and took care of themselves as he approached their spot on the list. Regardless, they were all in the *"Done"* category now.

As we made our way to the separation point on the original list, I wondered how we could make it past the wall of disbelief. Before I could come up with a profound strategy, Billy jumped the wall and said, *"The rest of this original list is in the bag!"*

"What do you mean?" I asked, actually a little disappointed that I didn't come up with something really cool and insightful to get him over the hump. *"You believe you can do all of those things now?"*

He went through every step asking himself if he believed. Every inquiry received an honest, confident, resounding, *"YES, I CAN."* Laughing with a sense of real joy and relief, Billy gave me a gift of insight. A mindset moment.

> *"From where I started, finishing this deal seemed impossible. Once I got started though, every step I took gave me a better look at the next one. I never had to convince myself that I needed to believe more. I worked within the belief that I had and it eventually got me all the way."*

He did not believe in his ability to accomplish the BIG goal and still yet, he got started. The action steps that were a little closer to him did not seem as big of a reach and he believed that he could make those happen. Instead of standing still, making himself feel guilty because he was not making progress toward the BIG goal, he picked a spot in-between and started moving.

Remember when I said that there were two reasons why I wasn't reaching my goals? One reason was purpose and you've got a firm understanding of it now. The other reason I mentioned was a lack of belief, just like

Billy. Both reasons are equally important, but they affect us in slightly different ways.

Purpose, as we covered, provides drive to keep us moving toward and through our goals. Without it, we putter out and fade off into the grass.

Belief is different in that a lack of belief will shut us down entirely or not even let us begin. Belief provides the confidence and courage to go forward. The lack of it paralyzes.

Why is a lack of belief so devastating? Take my example of mirroring the goals of more experienced colleagues. Assume I am a new runner and I mirror the goals of more experienced runners. Gwen, who finished the Boston Marathon last year in 3 hours 15 minutes, has a goal to finish it this year in less than 3 hours. Her level of belief that she can attain that goal is probably high.

If I mirror Gwen and set a goal to finish the Boston Marathon in under 3 hours after finishing my first ever mile in 8 minutes, where is my belief likely to be? Without the belief that I could get there, I would freeze. Taking the first step is impossible because one fear after another pops into the path.

- Fear of failure

- Fear of success

- Fear of looking stupid

- Fear of admitting I am scared

It doesn't really matter what the fears are. It only matters that the goal is so far beyond the level of belief that no progress toward it happens. By the way, that is all that fear is, a lack of belief.

Ever had a goal that intimidated you into staying put? If so, your lack of belief took the lead in your reaction. Let's look at belief and how we can turn it in our favor.

Belief often seems mystical because of its use to describe religion. I would like to simplify it just a bit for our purposes and make it more practical.

Belief is something that you accept as true even though you don't have any immediate, personal knowledge that confirms its validity.

Immediate personal knowledge means something that you have experienced, first-hand, through one of your physical senses. If you have experienced something in this way, it is not belief, its knowledge.

C.S. Lewis said that we do not BELIEVE in 2+2=4 or the noonday sun. We know those things.

Belief exists outside of what we know. It can be just outside of our personal knowledge or way beyond the bounds. Either way, we have to rely on the experiences of others, or what we can reason out of our knowledge and assumptions, to establish belief.

The degree to which you believe in something determines the level of action and risk you will take toward it. This is a crucial point as we move forward:

Your level of belief in something determines the level of action and risk you will take toward it.

In order to take steps toward our goals, we must believe we can get there. If the goal is too far beyond our belief level, we will sit still, contemplate, and worry over what might happen, instead of taking steps toward the accomplishment.

We are much better off to move toward a small goal than to sit motionless while we consider a BIG goal. The key is to get moving. How?

For starters, we must find where our belief touches the vision or goal. As you saw with Billy, if your belief and vision are not connected, you go nowhere. The vision you have crafted so far is a wonderful tool, but it will get you nowhere if it's out of touch with your belief.

Let's shift gears into a mini goal setting drill to help you understand.

Back to the running goal example. If I crafted a crystal clear picture of finishing the Boston Marathon in under 3 hours and defined my significant purpose for doing it, I next need to become aware of my belief level. The question is simple.

"Do I believe that I can finish this year's Boston Marathon in less than 3 hours?"

If the answer is anything other than a resounding, confident, and honest, *"YES,"* we need to do some work. To start, take the goal and break it down.

> Where are you now? Can run 1 mile in 8 minutes.

> Where do you want to be? Finish this year's Boston Marathon in under 3 hours.

Now we map the steps back from the big goal to where you are. These should be big steps at first. You can break it down to smaller steps later.

- Qualify by finishing a marathon in 3 hours and 45 minutes

- Finish a marathon

- Develop endurance for a marathon

- Finish a half-marathon

- Develop endurance for a half-marathon

- Finish a 10k

- Finish a 5K

- Run 2 miles

- Run one mile in less than 7 minutes

You get the idea… big intervals. Bring it back until you are just outside of what you know. The goal is close enough to touch, but not quite in your grasp.

Resume the awareness process for your belief level starting with the item just out of your grasp.

"Do I believe that I can run one mile in less than 7 minutes?"

If a resounding, confident, and honest *"YES"*…

"Do I believe that I can run 2 miles?"

If a resounding, confident, and honest *"YES"*…

"Do I believe…" until you find the place that you freeze. You don't really, truly believe that you can accomplish the mark. You'll know when that is. From that point, take one step back and you'll have found your point of focus.

I have found this method to be amazingly effective for everyone from CEO's of Fortune 100 companies to 3rd grade basketball players. A big reason for its power is that it builds belief without the need to play head games.

In addition, it gets us closer to our major goals without the fear and frustration associated with overwhelm. We get to move in confident, manageable strides.

What happens along the way

It doesn't matter to me if the place that your belief and vision meet is no farther away than the very edge of your knowledge. So long as it is out of that comfort zone, you'll grow by getting there.

If the only place that I have enough belief to feel confident is in running a mile in less than 7 minutes, that's where I start. I set aside the idea of the Boston Marathon all the way down to running 2 miles. I only focus on running one mile in less than 7 minutes. I take my first step and work toward that goal.

When I get there, I raise my head up and look at the next hurdle on my goal map. How do I feel about it now? Maybe I think, *"no sweat!"* Maybe I think, *"two miles still scares me, but 1 ½ miles is totally doable."* So that's my next focus.

Once I've grown far enough to achieve 1 ½ miles, *"two seems like a breeze... and you know what? A 5k is only one mile more. A 10k makes my stomach hurt just to think about it though."*

I focus on the 5k and get my butt moving. See where is this headed? The Boston Marathon, that's where! Or wherever the end of the rainbow is for you. It's pointless to try and convince ourselves to believe more. Instead, use what you have and nurture it.

You and I have both seen incredible examples of people accomplishing unbelievable feats of strength and courage. Old grannies lifting cars off their grandchildren and stuff like that. If you had asked them the logical question beforehand, *"can you lift that car,"* of course they would have said, *"No. "*

Their purpose was so strong in that moment of urgency though, they were able to suspend belief to accomplish what they needed to do.

For our everyday lives; however, we shouldn't rely on dramatic and extreme circumstances to move us past our level of belief. We can't effectively rely on continual leaps of faith to get where we want to go. We need simple, reliable, and repeatable steps to make life easier.

Day-to-day movements that take the elephants and reduce them to bite-sized chunks of belief.

To find the place that your vision and purpose touch your level of belief, use the following action guide.

> **Big vision** – write your vision or goal here

> **Why is it important** – write your purpose for completing the goal

> **Steps to get there** – list out the necessary steps to get there. Big steps, not minutiae

> **First step outside of your experience** – identify the first step that is beyond anything you've ever done before

> **Confirm your belief** – ask yourself, "do I believe that I can accomplish this step?"

If the answer is a truthful, "YES!" Move on to the next step.

Repeat until you freeze – when you hit the point that you cannot honestly answer, yes to accomplishment; go back to the previous step and focus your energy there.

Now that your vision and belief align, your next step is conquering the opportunities before you. *Let's Go!*

Mindset Moment
Nurture your current level of belief
and let it grow naturally.

Chapter 12

S.W.I.T.C.H.

CONQUER -
A Bias For Action

Take a deep breath. The work you've done to this point can be exhausting if you've never walked this path. Most people have never considered how they want their life to look, let alone what their purpose for achieving it is.

Just the exercise of coming face-to-face with your level of belief is enough to frighten the lighthearted. After all, belief is directly linked to fear and facing our fears ranks right up there with dental work.

Then again, you might have breezed through the previous exercises because you've done similar work before.

Regardless of your result to this point, it will all be for naught if we do not make something happen. We need Action!

As we will soon cover, what you have done so far, qualifies as action. And as you come to understand the Action Matrix you'll see that the action required for vision, purpose, and belief will only get you started. It will not create success. This is where we separate the "talkers" from the "doers."

History is full of people that can talk a good game but don't put their words into action. In the field of personal development, I constantly see individuals that love the idea of self-growth and "getting better." They read the books, attend the programs, and know exactly what they need to do to make their lives extraordinary. But they don't do it.

It's as if they think wanting the growth is enough to make it happen. They gravitate to the techniques and philosophies that are very thought-oriented and use them as a shield.

Thinking and talking about personal improvement is what this group really loves, not actually growing as a person. This happened most recently around the movie, *The Secret*, and the Law of Attraction.

The movie was so well produced and so entertaining, millions tuned in to the idea, *thoughts become things.* It is an exciting and motivating thought, especially for those that like to think and not act.

Several hucksters and overnight gurus jumped directly at the thinking group with one product after another centering around the Law of Attraction. Most of them claimed that *The Secret* was missing a vital piece to make the Law of Attraction work...*ACTION.*

In defense of the movie, they did talk about action in multiple places. I have often wondered if those gurus actually watched the movie they bashed.

I personally believe in Attraction and feel that *The Secret,* while flawed in many ways, was on the front-end of a new wave of awareness of which the world was in desperate need. There is now a fresh sense of possibility among a greater number of people and I believe that movie is a big reason why.

With that said, I also want to make it clear that I don't believe the Law of Attraction is a very useful tool for teaching people how to be successful.

If you are someone that believes in the Law of Attraction, relax. Nothing we've covered so far, or will cover from this point forward, stands in contradiction to Attraction. Every Element of Personal Choice gives you a practical, non-*"woo woo"* tool to harness Attraction.

If you are someone that resists the ideas taught in *The Secret* and the Law of Attraction, relax. Nothing we've covered so far, or will cover from this point forward, requires you to believe in Attraction. I have not and won't ask you focus on your vibration or give your power over to the Universe. Everything in the S.W.I.T.C.H. is practical, straightforward, and keeps your feet on the ground. Which brings us back to Conquering what we want and taking Action.

Think of what we are doing together as building your perfect vehicle to get you to the life you desire. Vision,

Purpose, and Belief is the body of the vehicle. Learning the different types of action, and how to put them to work for you, is how you drive this vehicle.

Types of action

I'm a type A. Big shocker, right? Up until my late 20's I thought that action was a one-dimensional requirement of success. I found friends and mentors to reinforce my attitude and keep my fire stoked.

Go, go, go... drive, drive, drive!

Make something happen!

Patience is for the weak!

If you weren't going mach-2 with your pants on fire, you weren't doing anything. I have mellowed my stance... slightly... since beginning the journey that I am guiding you through now. What I have come to understand from the guidance of my mentors and all of the people I have studied, action comes in more than one shape and size.

The ACTION Matrix

Inner Action

We'll understand action best by placing the four types of action in a 2x2 grid. In the top left square, we put Inner actions. This type has dominated this book so far. Inner actions are also the ones that I personally neglected for so many years.

Inner Actions **Contemplative** **Planning** **Evaluating** **Feeling**	

Inner actions represent the contemplating, planning, evaluating, and feeling aspects of life.

You are engaged in Inner actions when you consider questions like,

"What do I want my life to look like,"

"Why is that important to me,"

"Did that attempt give me the results I wanted,"

"How can I make it better?"

The benefit of Inner actions is that they can give you a significant advantage when carrying out your plans. Just like creating a vision of your ideal life puts your mind in motion toward it, planning your next move gives your mind the intended result. Inner actions also carry with them a warning.

Inner action alone does not yield results.

There is a tendency to stay in our heads when faced with a big task. We have an advantage over that problem because this S.W.I.T.C.H. structure gets us moving. However, please be aware of getting into an inner action groove… and turning it into a rut. We avoid that issue by converting our inner actions to outer actions.

Outer Actions

Outer action goes into the lower right quadrant of the grid. As the opposing item to inner actions, outer provides the only complement.

Inner Actions	
	Outer Actions **Doing** **Writing** **Stepping** **Progress**

If you have followed the exercises in this book, you've already taken outer actions, though they might not be what you're used to. Taking your mental vision and committing it to paper. Writing out the answers to questions on your way to a purpose statement. Mapping back the steps needed to attain your big vision during the belief exercise.

All of these things are outer actions. We need the outer actions we are more accustomed to as well. Planning the number of miles you'll run is one thing. Actually running them is where we make progress.

I used to think that outer actions would make everything better. Even if I didn't know what I needed to do, as long as I was moving, something good would happen. For the most part, I still believe that.

Movement is the primary goal of life. Brilliant ideas are nothing if they stay in someone's head. A mediocre mind that is willing to execute an idea brings far more health, wealth, and happiness than a first rate intellect who never puts an idea in motion.

Do something!

To make those outer actions really pay off though, you must combine them with inner actions. This is the give and give of constant improvement. If you take a moment and consider the best way to accomplish a task before setting into it, you are likely to have more success. If after an outer action is complete, you take a moment and evaluate the result for ways to improve, you've entered the cycle of greatness.

Putting inner and outer actions together in a cycle of constant improvement takes you to a life of uncommon success.

Obvious Actions

I prefer to put our next category in the upper right square of the grid. In this position, Obvious Actions interact with Inner and Outer actions equally well. This is the beginning of the Action Matrix I referred to earlier.

Inner Actions	*Obvious Actions* **Conscious** **Linear** **Left-Right-Left** **Planned**
	Outer Actions

Obvious actions give more form to inner and outer,

though they may require less explanations because... they're obvious.

Put another way, they are linear actions. For an inner-obvious action, you could begin by forming your vision. At this point in the book, you know that to have success in any area of your life, you need to know what success looks like. So, you craft your vision. It's an obvious action that happens internally.

The next obvious action with vision is to write it down so you can further activate your subconscious mind. Writing your vision makes it an outer-obvious action.

You do the same with Purpose, Belief, and so on. Each time you build momentum. No single step is too overwhelming or demanding and each step feels easier and more satisfying.

If you want to start your own business. An inner-obvious action is to consider what you want to do. What are your interests and skills? How would you finance the start-up?

The outer-obvious actions take the form of actualizing the inner-actions. Researching your potential market. Calculating a pro-forma and budget.

Obvious actions are planned and executed as such.

Intuitive Actions

Completing the Action Matrix is Intuitive action. We place it in the lower left quadrant... *because that's the only space left...* and because it sets opposed to Obvious action as its complement. This position allows Intuitive to interact with Inner and Outer in the same way and give you the full spectrum of awareness.

Inner Actions	Obvious Actions
Intuitive Actions **Subconscious** **Organic** **Spontaneous** **Soul Breaths**	**Outer Actions**

Intuitive actions often confuse and intimidate people at first blush. To clear the smoke and demystify, just understand that you've already taken intuitive actions.

Some of the most common come in the form of impulse buys. Another might been to call a friend unexpectedly or check your child's car seat again before pulling out of the drive.

The concept of a mother's intuition is driven by exactly what we are learning here. Mothers have a distinct purpose in this world; to protect, care, and nurture their family.

With such an emotionally charged and vivid picture of success in mind, her subconscious is going to look for ways to protect, care and nurture.

- She gets a mental cue that the kids are "in to something" they aren't supposed to be.

- There is something important that her college student isn't telling her... so she pushes a little more.

- She decides to check the lock on the back door... just in case... and finds that it's unlocked.

Do you see the value of an intuitive action?

The lesson is this same kind of intuition is available in every area of your life. The vision, purpose, and belief exercises set you up to harness the intuitive sense. Harness because it is already working, you just need to guide its power. Your job is to decide quickly on the validity of an intuitive nudge and act accordingly.

When you recognize an intuitive action presenting itself, use your purpose to decide on your action.

"What is the action that I'm being offered in this moment?"

"Is it in alignment with my purpose?"

If YES, take it and don't hesitate. Live in the moment and let your soul breath.

If NO, back away. Often, you can just let it move away without any issues. Sometimes you will need to select an alternate way around. Either way, you are honoring your purpose and realizing your vision.

Busy vs. productive

More than likely, the ideas of taking action are old-hat to you. So let's give them some structure that allows you to make them even more productive.

First, let's make a distinction between two types of work that didn't make it on to the Action Matrix: Busy work and Productive work.

Productive work is the stuff that moves you toward your goal in a material way. Busy work is everything else. Most of us can stay busy all day, every day. To have the life you deserve, you want to be productive instead.

Once you have indentified the steps toward a goal and the actions needed in those steps, you can evaluate who needs to do them.

That's right… just because something needs to be done, doesn't mean you have to be the one doing it. Honestly evaluate if there is someone else that could take the task and free you up for other actions your skills and talents are best suited for.

Take the focus point you arrived at in the Belief exercise. Now take all of the steps, in-between where you are and your first focus point, and break those into smaller action steps. The things needing completion in order to reach the focus point.

List them by priority or chronological order. Whichever is most appropriate.

Then, beside each action item, place an IO for Inner-Obvious or an OO for Outer-Obvious.

Now pick an action item and do it. Too simple again, I know. But the easiest thing to do right now is get moving. Even if it is only a small step in your eyes, it might be the most important step in your life. Just one. Then look around and see how you feel about the next step.

Inner/Outer Ratio

One thing to add, to help you avoid the Inner action trap of Analysis Paralysis, is to operate with a good ratio. Plan your action items with a ratio of no more than two inner actions for every outer action. This keeps you physically moving toward your goals.

When you consider a step, identify what type it is. Make sure that the ratio is right and get moving. When in doubt, go with an outer action.

The Movement Mirage

Another thing to watch for is the illusion of movement *(I used to spend so much time in this trap that I bought a condo)*. When people start taking this information and using it as intended, there is a surge of emotion and excitement.

The ideas and direction created are so powerful that we want to share everything we are going through. A swell of energy builds and needs to find an outlet. So we tell others what's going on.

We communicate our ideas and goals to others with enthusiasm and detail, so much so that we feel like we are actually making progress. Every time we tell someone about our goal, we leak the energy we need to make it reality.

Remember that our subconscious feeds on pictures and emotion. If we are communicating with great detail and emotion, our subconscious gets the same high as if we were really doing something. It's a set up and a trap. Don't fall into it.

Instead, focus on getting at least 75-80% of your goal accomplished before telling anyone about it. Results speak for themselves and are so much more impressive than ideas.

Of course, if there is someone that is necessary for your goal, you'll need to share some things with them. Only share what you must though. *Resist the urge to blab.* Let your energy escape into results.

Earlier I referred to your work in this book as building your vehicle to success. Vision, Purpose, and Belief form the body and motor, while Action represents how you drive. Forgiveness makes sure we are driving without the brakes on and free of obstacles.

Common knowledge would say that with those pieces in place, we're done. Common is what we are working to distance ourselves from.

The goal of this book, of flipping the SWITCH, is uncommon success.

Just like the sleek and beautiful convertible on the showroom floor, your mindset is handcrafted to take you anywhere you want to go. But no matter how gorgeous and powerful the car or your mindset might be, they won't go anywhere without ... *FUEL!*

Mindset Moment
Any Action is better than none,
but the RIGHT Actions give you a
knee-bending life.

Chapter 13

S.W.I.T.C.H.

Honor -
Feel the Gratitude

Your mindset is now a high-performance machine and high-performance machines demand the highest quality fuel. Fortunately for us, the best fuel available for your mindset is in abundant supply and completely at your disposal. It's Gratitude.

Gratitude performs like a high-octane fuel when placed into a machine like your mindset. Everything comes alive and burns within you. Your desires seem to rush toward you as your soul breaths through every available outlet.

Without gratitude, you can still accomplish a certain level of success. I have seen it and done it more times than I care to count. It never lasts though. Success without gratitude leaves you unsatisfied and thinking that nothing is ever good enough.

The worst side effect of success without gratitude is that you completely undervalue yourself. When nothing else is good enough, neither are you. You discount your contributions, ignore your needs, and constantly find what is wrong in the middle of everything that is right.

We all have a person in our life that lacks gratitude. They always find something to complain about regardless of how good things are. Nothing is ever good enough and there is always something wrong with every situation. If you do not think you have any of those people around you…you're probably the person.

The real problem is not just the complaining. A lack of gratitude can derail your entire life and cost you what is most precious.

Gary and I had known each other for more than 10 years. When he called me on that Tuesday afternoon, he was sobbing and near hysterical.

"I don't know what I'm going to do…I'm such an idiot," he began, without explaining anything.

"What do you mean? What's going on?" I asked.

"I cheated on Christy and she knows. She hasn't done it yet, but she might take the kids and leave…what am I going to do?"

After a few minutes to calm down, he gave me some details and perspective as to what happened and where things stood.

Gary and Christy had a young family and he traveled a lot for his job. He had traveled extensively for most of their marriage and was always faithful without any problems. During the past year though, their relationship felt tense.

Gary felt like Christy resented his travel while she stayed home. In his mind, she did not appreciate what he was doing and was not supporting him in growing his career. Instead of talking about it with her, he held it in.

With those emotions bottled up, he found himself daydreaming about the appreciation he desired. Since he traveled so often, his supporting environment was work and all of his daydreams centered on work.

Instead of the visions of a happy, loving family that used to fill his head, he thought of running the company and people revering him for his brilliance. *Cue the train wreck.*

On yet another extended trip, Gary met a colleague that found him fascinating. She talked about his business acumen and how people responded to him. He felt 10-feet tall and important. Though there was no physical relationship, the mental affair had started.

Three months later, knowing not to, Gary allowed himself to get into a compromising situation and the impending physical encounter happened.

What is it about major events that change our perspective on life? A near death experience, losing a loved one, financial ruin…they all hit people like a ton of bricks and make them see life more clearly. At least for a little bit.

Major events are game changers because people lack awareness of what is going on around them. They lack one or more pieces of their mindset, which puts them in a tailspin until they crash.

The impact seems to clear their vision for a brief period and they really understand what life is about. Immediately after his crash, Gary was seeing clearly for the first time in over a year.

His realization of how much his family meant to him caused a deeper awareness of what lead to the affair. When he felt unappreciated, Gary instantly took his mind to *"what is wrong,"* without giving any consideration to *"what is right."* By focusing entirely on the lack in his life, he pushed the good and great elements out of sight.

Though painful, I asked Gary to list all of the things that were right about his life when he began to feel the tension in his marriage. At the end of 20 minutes and sobbing again, he admitted not thinking about those things at all during the past year. All of his thoughts were about filling voids, not honoring what was already there. His lack of gratitude threatened to wreck his life.

In short, your life without gratitude is misery. I meet people all the time who want to know how to perform better. When we actually dig down to what they want right away, we find out they just want to be happier. That's when I smile and let them in on a little secret that the pharmaceutical industry hates.

I can put your mind in a natural state of happy, instantly! No prescriptions or drugs of any sort. The secret? Find gratitude and honor what you love in your life.

It's too simple, I know. But it's the God's honest truth. Try it right now. Think of something you love that you can honestly say, *"I'm grateful to have that in my life."* As soon as that picture forms in your mind... you smile. At least a little.

I put it to the test again recently at my maternal grandma's funeral. In the midst of the visitation, just before the service, and while visiting with family afterward I found myself smiling and chuckling from time-to-time. My mind was playing a never-ending loop of great memories of me and my grandma.

Waiting for the school bus at her house on cold mornings. She had me lie next to the heating vent and put a blanket over me that filled up like a tent when the heat came on.

During the summer, she held a perpetual yard sale. She would let me sell the African Violets that she grew in her little greenhouse for half the gross. Plus, I got a high-five for every sale.

I would let the feelings of loss and hurt have their turn, but they were not allowed to rule. The gratitude of her impact on my life held sway because I chose for it to. Some of my family was having a much more difficult time.

As we talked, I never told them to change their minds or how they were thinking. Regardless of how depressed they wanted to be about the loss, I have no right to force them out of it. I did ask them to let their soul breathe though. Not with that direct question, but by asking them to share with me their fondest memory.

In an instant, they lit up. They would tell the story with vivid detail and heroic emotion. They laughed with genuine joy and celebrated the moment, both past and present. When they finished, you could see a noticeable difference in their demeanor.

I asked them, like I ask my clients, what they were feeling in their bodies at that moment. After a moment of consideration, they responded with a variety of physical sensations. Mostly tingles in the arms or back. Some noticed a warming sensation in their chest or stomach. Every one of them noticed something.

That is the often-overlooked gift of gratitude. I wondered for years, how can I recreate and lock-in that happiness and emotional high I get from gratitude? What I finally realized is that the tools I sought were already built-in.

When we experience gratitude, it goes beyond the emotional state. If we heighten our awareness, we start to notice that our bodies reflect the emotion in physical form. Give it a try.

Bring back the thought from earlier of something for which you are sincerely grateful. Close your eyes and color the picture with as much detail as possible. The lighting, sounds, and smells. Now as you hold that picture, person, event, place, in your mind... tune in to what is going on with your body.

- Is there a tingling in the top of your arms?

- Do you feel a little short of breath?

- Butterflies in your stomach?

- Does your scalp tighten up slightly?

- Maybe a small chill runs up you back?

Whatever it is, I guarantee that something is there. Find it and get comfortable with its presence. This sensation is the magic portal to instant happiness and the never-ending supply of fuel for your success machine.

Please don't think that I'm slipping into a *"think it and it will happen"* mentality either. Not even close. Where we are headed is the mastery of a fantastic and practical tool that you can use to amplify your short-term success and lock it in for the long-term.

Remember, I travel in the same circles as the people that have rode *The Secret* and the law of attraction into the ground. I understand what comes into most people's minds when they begin to hear about the benefits of gratitude.

The intent for teaching you gratitude as a tool is more technical than fantasy. Sorry if fantasy is what you were looking for. I use gratitude to not only make you feel better, but to correct one of the largest falsehoods that has come out of the self-help industry in the last 50 years. The idea of convincing yourself that something has happened when it hasn't. Sometimes called, Fake-It-Till-You-Make-It.

Have you ever tried to hold a vision of what it is you want and tell yourself, *"I've already got it,"* when you know you don't? How does your brain react to that?

You: *"I have a house on the beach and I'm financially independent."*

Brain: *"No you don't. You're broke, work too much at a job you hate, and you've never seen the ocean."*

You: *"I have all the free time I want and travel extensively with my family."*

Brain: *"Your kids see the baby-sitter more than they see you. Besides, when's the last time you went somewhere with your family that didn't involve an awkward holiday?"*

Our brains are relentless; they know all our secrets because *that's* where we keep them! Trying to convince yourself that something *is*, when your brain is keenly aware that it *isn't*, has probably done more harm than good.

The intent of the fake-it-till-you-make-it exercise was to find a way to activate your subconscious mind toward the fulfillment of the vision. We have talked about the need for that to happen so I am not discounting the intent at all. The problem is that it tends to work in the opposite direction. Making us feel guilty and stupid for trying to bend reality.

We are going to use gratitude and full transparency to accomplish what fake-it-till-you-make-it never could.

Bring emotion to your vision

Recall the physical sensations you noticed while in a state of gratitude. Spend just a moment feeling. At any point while you are in this state of gratitude, do you hear your mind telling you the feeling isn't real? Of course not, because it is real. Your brain has no reason to fight you on this.

You are allowed to fully enjoy and absorb the experience because it does not trigger any of the brain's defenses. You are experiencing a piece of your current reality, which puts the emotion and vision in alignment. Why is that important?

Have you noticed that when you are consciously grateful for something, you tend to get more of it? That is because you have the perfect combination feeding your subconscious mind. You clearly detail the images of what you currently have and match those details with the appropriate emotion. Your subconscious receives the input and says, *"I obviously like this thing that I'm seeing... guess I ought to have more of it."*

The pattern is perfect. So let's use that to our further advantage. Okay?

Tying a knot

Fully engage the images and emotions of something for which you are grateful. What are the physical sensations you experience while seeing those things in your mind?

Now switch to your big vision. See the picture of your ideal life fully detailed. The colors, the sounds, and smells... you aren't trying to convince yourself that you already have the result...just enjoy the details like you enjoy a movie.

Then casually come back to your picture of gratitude. Anticipate the physical sensations and welcome them as they come back. Feel them deeply.

Once you've locked-in the sensations again, come back to your big vision. See if the sensations of gratitude stay with you even though you're in your big vision.

Back and forth you go. Gratitude. Vision. Gratitude. Allow the two to blend. The goal is to feel the physical sensations of gratitude while holding the image of your big vision. And just in case you're wondering... yes, this is totally legal.

Practice this daily. It only takes a few minutes and can become one of your favorite times of day. Relax and consider it a mini vacation.

Tapping into that unending supply of fuel is a real trip. Gratitude was the biggest mindset moment of my early journey. Understanding how to use what I already possessed to acquire what I desired gave me a new sense of control and confidence.

Trouble finding gratitude

You should also know that finding gratitude was not easy for me to do at one point in my life. I was as low as I had ever been in many ways.

- I weighed 235 lbs on a 5'8" frame.

- My triglycerides (blood fat) were three times the high limit.

- My boss and mentor fired me from the highest paying job I had ever held.

Not the end of the world perhaps, but certainly not the life I wanted. The Elements of Personal Choice and my work surrounding mindset were still forming, but I knew there was a way forward from where I stood. The best way to turn my head in the right direction was finding gratitude. But where?

I did not see anything deserving of gratitude. That seemed too optimistic. Instead of pushing myself to get in a positive state of mind, I used my dominant emotion in that moment: loss.

"What is the one thing that would send me over edge if I lost it?"

The answer was easy. My family. I had not lost them yet and felt my entire body swell with emotion as they filled my mind. It was there that I found gratitude.

Just in case you find yourself in a similar place, consider my example. You cannot lose something that you do not have. If you have something that you are afraid of losing, this means it is important to you. If it's important and you have it, you can be grateful!

Please do not take this as semantics. Finding gratitude, no matter where you are, is critical to your success and happiness. Gratitude keeps you in the moment and directs you toward more for which to be grateful.

For me, the realization of gratitude was profound. This down moment in my life also provided the backdrop to bring a full understanding of how the Elements of Personal Choice integrate to form our mindsets. Having the Elements individually is not enough. We have to know how to bring them together.

> *Mindset Moment*
> *Honoring the current good in your life is the quickest way to increase the amount of good you receive.*

Chapter 14

Now that you've flipped the S.W.I.T.C.H.

The Questions Answered

You've walked through all of the Elements of Personal Choice individually and seen their importance. Each one brings strength and stability to your mindset, but it takes all of them to enjoy life at its fullest.

Understanding how to use the Elements together puts you in the rarified air of the world's most successful and gives you the capability to handle any situation the world can offer. You can flip the SWITCH.

When I set out on my journey to unravel the mystery of mindset, I received a gift from the people around me. The questions written on the back of the yellow evaluation cards after my first presentation guided me. In each interview or coaching session, I looked for clues to answer those questions.

Now, with all seven Elements in place, we revisit those questions and show you how you can answer each. The exercise of answering these questions shows you how to approach any situation you will ever face.

Advanced warning: You will notice some redundancy in how we approach these questions. I would apologize but that would undercut the point. When we look at how to solve problems, redundancy is good. If we can approach every issue with the same set of tools, we get *really good* with those tools and nothing intimidates. Breathe easy and get used to the process.

- Isn't desire enough?

- Why doesn't goal setting work for everyone?

- Can I really "fake it till I make it?"

- Can personal and financial success exist together?

- Why do similar people get such different results?

- Why do I fall back after making such progress?

- How do I know what I'm afraid of and make it go away?

- Why does my self-confidence fluctuate so much?

- I've failed before, why won't it happen again?

- Why can't I get rid of negative thoughts?

- How do I find my life's purpose?

- Why do I procrastinate?

- Is it really possible for anyone to be successful?

Isn't desire enough?

Born of frustration, this question comes from the misconception, *"if you want something bad enough you'll get it."* People burn out from this notion all of the time. You've discovered in the previous chapters, desire can seed accomplishment but it can't make it happen.

The most common issues I've found with those asking this question are belief and purpose. Just because you have a burning desire to achieve or obtain something doesn't mean that you believe you can get there. I've come to understand prolonged desire as a minor form of despair for many people.

They see something they want and fixate on the prize. Because of their lack of belief, they delay taking the necessary steps to get there. Combine the obsession with the crippling lack of belief and you get depression.

Pent-up desire without action toward the desire is similar to competing in a car race in neutral. The flag drops, you slam on the gas, and go nowhere. Without putting the car in gear, you make a lot of noise, make zero progress, and burn up. How's your self-esteem in that scenario?

There is another side to action and desire, which changed my perspective forever. My friend and colleague, Scott, was a hard driving guy. Our shared attitude toward massive amounts of desire, focus, and action made us very compatible. He had set his sights on becoming the youngest person in his company to receive a national-level promotion and I was set to cheer him on.

To watch him from the outside was remarkable. He took after the goal like a man possessed. His desire to achieve burned like a torch and all of his attention turned to the goal. It looked like his single-minded desire was indeed enough to make it happen.

Since I was closer to the situation than most, my vantage point revealed a few more things. Scott stayed at the office continually. His house was for showering and a change of clothes. His health began to slip from improper amounts of sleep and poor nutrition.

Within four months of setting his goal, his fiancé called off the engagement and left. When I asked him about the break-up, he blamed her for not supporting him in his goal. *"She just didn't believe in me and my vision,"* he said.

"So what exactly is your vision," I asked. He started to swell up and get confrontational then he realized, he could not answer the question. Scott had not taken the time to consider what he wanted his life to look like when he set out for the promotion.

His desire for the result was so strong it made him unconscious to the rest of his life. All he knew was the promotion. His sight had narrowed to the point that he couldn't see any other part of life around the promotion.

Did that mean he had to give up his goal to bring his bigger life back? No. But he did have to decide exactly what he wanted and get conscious about the position the promotion would take. With a little guidance and tough love, he found it easy to align the pieces of the life he desired.

As we discussed in the chapter on Trust, to achieve your big goals you have to get started. It is more productive to make progress toward a smaller goal than to stand paralyzed by a bigger one. When you find your desire for something is white hot, but you aren't getting there, go through the belief exercise and find the place where your vision and belief meet. Get started toward the smaller goal and let the process take over.

The other side of the desire coin is purpose. Unlike with belief, when we lack purpose toward something we desire we'll actually get started. Our problems come because we don't maintain our momentum.

If you've ever seen magnesium burn, you've seen what I mean. Magnesium is a metal and when lit it produces an amazingly bright light. Just as you think the light could damage your eyes from its brilliance…it's gone.

When we take off after a goal or objective with huge desire, we look and feel like the magnesium when first lit. Brilliant, powerful, and impressive. Then, poof! Just like the magnesium, we fizzle out and disappear.

Perhaps things got difficult. Because we lacked a strong purpose to sustain our efforts, we fade. This is especially frustrating because we seldom realize why we let down.

With any goal, especially one with a high-level of desire, make sure you understand and establish your purpose. The simplest exercise is 5 Deep. Ask yourself, *"Why am I pursuing this goal?"* Then dig down five layers to find a significant purpose. If your goal isn't worth the exercise, it isn't worth your time.

Why doesn't goal setting work for everyone?

I want to clear something up real quick. Earlier I said that bad goals are a plague on society. I also said, the S.M.A.R.T. method of goal setting wasn't enough. Neither of those things mean that I don't believe in traditional goal setting models or goals in general.

I believe goals are very important and every successful person I've ever met or studied makes a regular practice of setting goals. Methods like S.M.A.R.T. are also very useful and make the goal setting process much easier and more systematic. I am not opposed to either.

But I strongly believe that traditional goal setting focuses in the wrong places and is incomplete. Most people do not have trouble with the structure of setting a goal. They fail because they don't choose the right goals or understand what must be in place to achieve a goal.

I've worked with countless people, myself included, who spend hours setting their goals, but never spend the time to figure out what it will look like or why they even want it. When asked, they don't believe they can accomplish the goal and are still hung up on the last goal they set and failed to reach.

When we decide to set a goal it's okay to begin with the goal itself. But when you have a goal in mind, the next step is not to worry about the S.M.A.R.T. structure. The first key is to take the goal through our S.W.I.T.C.H. process and see if it is the right goal.

Can you SEE IT? Do you have a clearly defined picture of the goal accomplished? Without a vision, you are less likely to recognize opportunities to realize the goal. Plus, when you expand your vision around the goal to other areas of your life, the fulfillment and satisfaction with the pursuit is much higher.

WHY do you want it? Take the time to go 5 Deep. Once you have dug down… is there a strong reason for the goal or has a different goal emerged? If a new, more important goal appeared, go back to SEE IT and get a clear vision.

Have you granted yourself IMMUNITY to pursue it full out? Are you questioning your ability to make it happen because of past failures? Are you willing to allow yourself to stub your toe, bloody your nose, and keep going without regret? Is there anything holding you back that has to do with the past and will you let it go?

Do you TRUST yourself? You see the vision and know why it's important. So do you believe that you can accomplish the end goal? Can you answer with a resounding, confident, and honest, "YES" to every step along the way? If not, find the place where your belief and vision meet.

Are you ready to CONQUER the steps? Regardless of your past, when the first four elements are in place, action is not a problem. Are you clear on the steps needed? When an intuitive action presents itself, will you check it against your purpose before acting? If the purpose aligns with the action, will you take it? You only need one step at a time.

HONOR your life as you go. Are you actively looking for gratitude in your life? Do you celebrate each small victory along the way? Each thing you celebrate will fuel your next steps to accomplishing your goal.

Do you see how the best-structured goal in the world is useless without this foundation in place? Good structure does not fix bad goals. Get the right goals in place for the right reasons and you will guarantee accomplishment.

Ultimately, you will find that your goals come from consciously engaging the Elements of Personal Choice. If you start without a goal and go through the S.W.I.T.C.H. process, you will find exciting, progressive goals are the natural bi-product. When a goal comes from your mindset, you always succeed.

Can I really
"fake it till I make it?"

Psychotic was the word I used to describe this practice earlier in the book. The entire idea of fake-it-till-you-make-it is flawed because you are "faking" the result hoping the cause will come into alignment. This is like acting as if your basement isn't flooded hoping your pipes will miraculously mend. I'm not saying it can't happen, but that isn't a high-percentage play.

Wanting to connect your vision with the right emotions is wonderful and productive, but not by trying to convince your brain, things are different than they are. Your subconscious mind is amazingly powerful. As I presented in the chapter on Honor, we only need to give the subconscious the right material and it will tie the two together on its own. No games.

The purpose of tying this subconscious knot between our vision and gratitude is so that the vision comes alive. With a clear, emotional picture, we can put the rest of the Elements in place and make something happen.

At this point, we can establish our Purpose to support our efforts. Next, we confirm our Belief and layout our Obvious Actions to get started. Our heightened awareness tunes us in to Intuitive Actions that get us closer to that vision and we are now able to recognize Forgiveness issues. They all work together without the need for vibrations and universal alignments that are out of your control.

Be true to yourself, always. If you are ever asked to do something that feels incongruent or like an attempt to lie to yourself, challenge it.

Can personal and financial success exist together?

The idea of balancing your professional and personal life is a fallacy for real fulfillment. In the popularized version of this notion, we are told to take what we have and attempt to spend equal amounts of time, manage our time, and guard certain areas like a pit bull. As with other mass movements, the focus is in the wrong place.

If you, like many of my clients, told me that you needed help balancing your life, I would need to ask you why. The answers are different for every person and reveal that most people view life-balance as something to achieve and maintain. How many other parts of your life stay the same for any length of time?

Our lives are dynamic and alive! They aren't the same from one week to the next and priorities are constantly shifting and evolving. If we attempt to stay "balanced" throughout, we end up short-changing ourselves in some area and begin to build resentment. We need something more fluid and engaging than balance.

I do not claim to grasp the intricacies of a musical performance, but there is something I know…music is not about balance. When you hear a symphony, the conductor does not strive to have all of the instruments in equal parts at all times. Some play soft, some play loud, and some don't play at all.

Instruments are asked to take different roles from one stanza to the next. It is how each instrument contributes to fulfilling the composer's vision of the whole that determines the beauty of the performance. You probably saw this coming, but our lives are the same way.

No one has only two parts of their life. If we only consider the popular notions of professional, health, spiritual, personal growth, family, friends, hobbies, etc. you can see that there are myriad areas to every life. I have heard experts separate nearly everything else away from professional as an attempt to simplify. How does that work?

- Separate health from professional and how effective are you?
- Personal growth from professional? You won't stay on top for long.
- Family from professional? Why are you working in the first place?

On and on we can go with only one point to make; every area of your life is dependent on the others. Some of them get greater time and attention, but not because they are more or less important. You give them different levels of energy because that is what is required to fulfill your vision for your life. This is where the answer to our question lies.

Can personal and financial success exist together? Absolutely! If that is the vision for your life.

Consider your life as the symphony. Before the first note is played, the composer has a purposeful vision for the result and lays it out in notes, sounds, moods, timing. Then the conductor receives the sheet music to bring it to life. In our case, the composer and conductor are the same. We take the role of creating and putting the vision into action.

Each section of instruments receives their role. The instruments do not dictate to the conductor or composer what their role will be. The percussionist doesn't say, *"Screw you maestro! I'm gonna bang on this tympani drum through the whole thing!"* He plays what he's told, when he's told.

When we start with the purposeful vision for what we want our lives to be, the various sections of our lives fall into their roles. We don't allow one area to dictate the roles of the rest or force an area to play smaller than it needs. We allow them all to play according to our vision.

When we do, the emotion, purpose, and passion pours out in everything we do. No matter how big or small the area or activity, it complements the whole with beautiful clarity and intention. And like the patrons that witness a virtuoso performance from the symphony, those that witness your life are in awe of the gifts and beauty you bring to the world.

Individuals define personal and financial success, not groups. Only you decide what constitutes winning, because you make the rules to the game. **What do you want your life to look like?** Start there and put everything else into its proper measure.

Why do similar people get such different results?

This question perplexed me for years. At first, the answer seemed obvious. *Because people are different...duh!* But as I gained deeper understanding about behavior and mindset, I started to see that the issue is much more complex.

First, like most of the self-improvement literature out there, the question focuses in the wrong place. *The results.* If we want to know why things turn out differently, we need to look back to the beginning. The mindset going in to an endeavor or event.

When a room full of people set nearly identical goals because it seems like the right thing to do, they are all doomed to failure. You have come to understand through this book that a goal is only a bi-product of a properly constructed mindset, not the starting point. Did those people ask themselves,

"Why do I want this goal?"

"Do I really believe I can accomplish the goal?"

"What will life look like when the goal is achieved?"

"Are there any issues from my past that could obstruct my path?"

Chances are, no. None of those questions were asked or answered and all of them are crucial to the result. Part of the complexity is any of the issues those questions address can derail someone's pursuit. There is not one, isolated answer as to why people end up with different experiences. That's why knowing and using all of the Elements of Personal Choice is so important.

Instead of getting caught up in a goal-setting hysteria, as was common in one of my old companies, set goals based on your purposeful vision. Yes, this is redundant. I warned you. But understanding this point is so important to having success and happiness.

We must begin with what we want our lives and businesses to look like and why we want them to look that way. Good goals are the child of those two, not the other way around. When your goals come from knowing what and why, their accomplishment is natural and fluid.

Let's take our attention from the fascination of why the same goal brings varied results for similar people. Instead, put your focus toward finding the right goals for you as an individual.

Why do I fall back after making such progress?

The sensation of falling is the oldest nightmare known to man. The sensation of returning to square one might be just as old and definitely more frustrating. Compounding the frustration is how most of us solve the problem by following the exact same routine that got us there to start with. Finally, we can break the cycle and address the potential causes to find out, which is breaking us down.

Starting at the top of the list of potential causes is lack of vision and awareness. This is the reason I referred to the problem as a sensation. Unless you know exactly where you started and have a clear vision for where you are going, how do you know if you're back where you started? You don't.

You might *feel* like you're starting over, but might very well be in a brand new place. If you lack vision, you don't really know what success looks like even if it's staring you in the face.

Next is purpose and gratitude. These two held the reins for me more than once and guided me right back to the beginning. I knew where I wanted to go and what it looked like, but never established a strong enough reason for being there.

For added effect, I didn't take the time to appreciate what was right about my life. All I knew was that it wasn't good enough. I had to have and be more.

The combined absence of purpose and gratitude is like trying to drive a car...with no steering wheel or gas! You can work your tail off trying to get somewhere and nothing happens. You feel like you are coming back to square one, but the truth is, you never left.

A common companion to any of these issues is the gradual disappearance of action. You simply stop doing the things you need to do. You get scared and back off or you lose interest. Regardless, the activity stops.

The other side of the action coin is filling all of your time doing the wrong things. This is one of the main symptoms people treat with time management. Instead of understanding what are the right things to do and why to do them, we manage our time so we can get more of the wrong things into our schedule. Welcome back to square one.

Follow the steps and the issue of falling back goes away.

How do I know what I'm afraid of and make it go away?

Stop me if you've heard this one…the question is looking in the wrong place. If we set about looking for fears, we'll find them. The issue of making them go away is complicated by our focus.

"Did you find the fear?"

"Yep."

"Okay. Make it go away… Is it still there?"

"Yep."

"Wow, you must really be afraid."

Einstein said that we can't solve a problem with the same thinking that created it. We can't rid ourselves of fears by focusing on fears. Fear is the absence of belief. Where you perceive fear, there is something that you don't believe.

Fear of the dark. You don't believe that you'll be safe in the dark.

Fear of failure. You don't believe people will respect you if you fail or you don't have the ability to complete the task.

Fear of success. You don't believe people will still like you if you succeed.

Pick what you think of as a fear and you can find the corresponding belief that makes it go away. Just like turning on a light makes the darkness disappear, belief renders fear obsolete. So let's stop looking for our fears and spend our energy establishing our belief.

As we've covered, this isn't about pushing for more belief. Our goal is to work within the belief we already have and let it expand naturally through accomplishment.

Look at the area in which you sense fear. Whether you have a distinct fear that is obvious to you or not, ask yourself a question.

"What belief is lacking that causes this feeling?"

Use the belief exercise to help pinpoint where your belief slacks. You'll know when you've found it because of the sensation of discovery. Now continue with the belief exercise and move your attention to within your circle of belief. By shifting focus, you operate in the light, and darkness can't exist in the light.

Why does my self-confidence fluctuate so much?

"One day I'm the top dog. The next, I'm the fire hydrant."

Remember that phrase from earlier? My client, Eric, is the one I first heard it from and I've been ripping it off every since. The sentiment conveyed is easy to understand and most people just smile and nod their heads when they hear the words. We all know how this feels.

Eric was just as normal as anyone when we met. He had a job that he didn't hate, but didn't love. Married for eight years with three kids and a cat. Mortgage, car payments, braces, etc. You get the picture. Vanilla.

The thing that brought Eric and I together was his dream of entrepreneurship. It's been my privilege to work with thousands of entrepreneurs and small business owners, and one of them suggested to Eric that we make his dream reality.

Our biggest hurdle to getting Eric off the ground was the number of times he had began and faded before. As soon as he started executing his plan, he got scared and backed off. The cycle was vicious and each time took a toll on his self-confidence.

At the time, I wasn't certain of the problem, but I had a few steps for us to work through. Vision was easy because he had tried before and knew what success would look like. When we talked about purpose though, I was a little surprised by his inability to respond. He had never considered *why* he wanted to own a business. There was no real reason underpinning the vision or effort.

Once we dug deep and figured out what he wanted from business ownership, everything changed. I'd like to tell you that he got started on his plan and now owns a successful company, but isn't the case.

When we figured out his purpose, we also figured out he could fulfill that purpose by keeping his current job. Yes, he could also fulfill the purpose by starting a company, but that wasn't really his dream. Eric wanted significance from his profession and to set a great example for his kids of dedication and accomplishment.

I encouraged him to share that purpose with his boss. Guess who was thrilled to hear Eric define some purpose and began helping him make it happen? The boss became his biggest cheerleader and took a direct interest in his growth.

It's no secret that I'm a huge fan of entrepreneurship because I am nearly unemployable myself due to my inability to punch a clock. That isn't because I think jobs are bad.

Business ownership provides *ME* what I want out of life. I didn't become a successful business owner and then figure out if it was right for me. I looked at what I wanted from life and why. Then I decided on the pieces to attain the vision and fulfill my purpose.

No, Eric does not own the company he works for, but he has the incredibly fulfilling life he wants. He knows what he wants from every aspect of life and doesn't have self-confidence issues any more. If he ever feels his confidence waiver, he centers himself by confirming his purpose. You can do the same.

Establish your purposeful vision before anything else. Then compare it with your current reality and decide what pieces fit and what pieces you'll have to get or get rid of. This is where all of the primary tools you've learned in this book begin to produce the secondary tools, like goal-setting.

When you know what you want and why, set a goal. Make it a S.M.A.R.T. goal if you want. There's nothing wrong with using the structure if your goal is good to start with.

Now establish your level of belief and take action. Remembering all the time to honor what is good in your life and be aware of your gratitude. If you are consciously moving toward your most fulfilling life, that by itself is something in which to be grateful.

When you know exactly where you're headed, self-confidence is in ample supply.

I've failed before, why won't it happen again?

I'm the best example I know for the perils of failure. My entire childhood and most of my adult life shows the effects of hanging on to failures and losing opportunities. It's difficult to grasp anything new when your hands are full of the past.

Past failure is a like the potent compounds used in prescription drugs. A little can have medicinal effects and make you better. Contact with huge amounts over prolonged periods will kill you.

The medicinal qualities of failure come from awareness. We look critically at the failure and pull the lessons for future improvement. Remember how the quality management systems work? This is the, *evaluate and plan for improvement* phase.

More importantly, we don't just evaluate failures for improvements. We also dissect the successes to see how we can get better. To look at it properly, we shouldn't even use failure or success as the labels. Everything in this phase is a result. We can get better from either.

Once we've found a way to improve, the lesson from the result, we let it go and move on. That's right. Let go of your successes too, and move on.

I can't speak for you, but for me, I always felt like I needed to hang on to my failures. It was a defense mechanism that didn't allow anyone to catch me off-guard and bring me down. If I kept my failures close and brought them up before anyone else could, somehow that was an advantage. Completely freaking psychotic!

Unfortunately, I've found that I'm not the only one. Millions of people hang on to the past as a way of keeping themselves from hurt or embarrassment. It's as if we use them to keep us from feeling too good about ourselves and out of harm's way. *God forbid we should feel TOO good about who we are!*

This is why I say, prolonged exposure will kill you. When we continue to hang on to the past, it gets in our system. It might not be noticeable at first, but eventually the effects start to surface. Our behaviors toward achieving change. The things we're willing to attempt suffer as well.

For me, it manifested as a deluded sense of protecting an image. As a teenager, I convinced myself that it was better to look like I didn't care than to lose while doing my best. If I could see that I wasn't going to win, wouldn't get an 'A', or the girl…I would pull up. Somewhere in that testosterone-plagued head of mine, it was better to look like I didn't give my best effort than it was to give my all in defeat.

Why didn't someone grab me by the shoulders and shake me?!

Giving your heart and soul to an endeavor is the only way to truly win. I have just as many stories of winning easily and not learning a thing. Regardless of the score, if you didn't get better, you lost. However, if you are better in any way, you've won.

The habits created by my attitude carried into adulthood and effected everything I touched. I didn't want to fail. My unconscious plan to prevent failure was to only engage in "sure wins" and never push the edge of what was possible. It never worked.

I was eventually outted as a closet failure by one of my distance mentors, Art Williams. Though I've yet to met Art, during one of the dozens of his taped speeches I kept in my car, he described the patterns in his life.

A pattern of holding back and not giving it his all.

A pattern that repeated into his adult life.

A pattern that proved toxic until he let go of the failures and decided that they did not equal his future.

It was like he was reading my mail! That was *my* pattern. I had never seen it before, but sure enough, there it was. Fearing my past, I hid from my present. I held a grudge against myself for attempting and failing.

How's that for dysfunctional? I secretly hated myself for being unwilling to risk more and despised myself for having ever risked in the first place. In order to change, I had to break that pattern. Enter forgiveness.

In the quiet of my room and the depths of my soul, I came face-to-face with every disappointment from my life.

- The kindergartner that sometimes colored outside of the lines when his best friend never seemed to.
- The second-grader in a new school that shrunk because he thought kids wouldn't like him if he was in an advanced reading group.
- The fifth-grader who missed a chance to have the prettiest girl in school as his girlfriend because people would find out he had never kissed a girl.
- The eighth-grader, at a new school with a chance to start over, that decided to deny his true self and take on the "cool kid" persona.
- The 16-year-old that didn't have the guts to ask an adult for advice when his girlfriend said she was pregnant.
- The 18-year-old that gave up baseball scholarships because he wouldn't ask his coach for help to secure one.
- The 22-year-old that partied himself into a hole because the resentment of his past left him empty.

On and on it went. I approached each demon, only to realize they weren't demons at all. They were scared, uneasy pieces of me that just wanted to feel at home. Their purpose wasn't to restrict my life or haunt me. They wanted to be forgiven, learned from, and welcomed as threads in the tapestry that is my life.

Bringing each one into the light and giving grace turned them from hidden weaknesses to conscious strengths. With every layer of forgiveness, I felt more alive. My head cleared and my heart freshened. For the first time, I could feel my soul breathe.

Your past does not equal your future. Past success does not equal future success. Past failure does not equal future failure. The lessons taken from each experience and the actions you take based on those lessons are the only real predictor.

When we look at failure, we have to learn and forgive. There is no future in resentment or guilt. Identify where you are stuck and find the block. Clear it out with whichever method of release you choose, but make sure to clear it. Your life depends on it.

Why can't I get rid of negative thoughts?

Optimist, pessimist, or realist? I've often wondered which one I am.

Optimists (I'm not talking about the civic organization) say they look for the good in life and think that things will turn out that way. In their estimation, pessimists are sad, pathetic people that only need a little sunshine in their lives to perk them up.

Pessimists claim they aren't looking for bad stuff, but figure it's going to turn out bad no matter what they do. To a pessimist, optimists are fruitcakes. Delusional Pollyannas who are entirely too perky and refuse to admit the world is a bad place, full of bad people.

Self-proclaimed realists, in my experience, are typically pessimists that don't want to be labeled as extreme. They consider both ends of the spectrum to be undesirable and prefer the safe, bath-water warm ground in the middle. Realists like to have access to the optimistic side of the wheel, but still reserve the right to be cynical of everyone's intentions.

There has never been a more perfect example of how mindset determines your view of the world than these three groups. It almost sounds like a setup for a joke.

An optimist, a pessimist, and a realist walk into a bar. The bartender pours each of them a beer and sets each mug with the handle pointing to the right of the drinker.

The optimist says, *"I'm left-handed and am so glad that you are encouraging me to develop my right hand's strength by positioning the mug this way."*

The realist says, *"I'm right-handed so the mug is positioned to my strength, but why should I be happy about that?"*

The pessimist says, *"It doesn't matter which way it's pointed. I'll probably die before I can drink it anyway."*

Okay, I know it's not a good joke, but it sets up my point. Everyone in the world can look at the exact same thing and get different impressions. Doubt me? Think of a political debate.

Two candidates. Everyone hears the same words. Then the pundits, analysts, and water cooler know-it-alls take over and deliver their take. I sometimes wonder if I watched the same debate. To make it worse, three people on the same show act like they all listened to something different. Everyone gets a different result. Why?

Knowing what you now know about mindset, you can see how this is possible. My mindset filters the input from the candidates and gives me the data I need to reinforce my internal picture of what is real. Yours does the same. Unless we are looking for the exact same things, our conscious minds will each receive different input.

This is why I say, good and bad are matters of perception. Every event has the potential to be good or bad. An event means nothing until we assign meaning. So what does that have to do with getting rid of negative thoughts? Everything.

First, you need to understand that you cannot get rid of negative thoughts. True story. Because everything has the potential to be either good or bad, every bit of input has both a negative and positive end. When the input hits our mindset, we have predetermined which end is presented to our conscious mind.

If you picture the bits of input as little batteries, you'll see what I mean. A battery has both a negative and positive end. If I turn the battery with the positive end pointing toward me, I haven't eliminated the negative. All I've done is focus on the positive.

You wouldn't want to eliminate the negative end anyway. It is the interaction between the two that creates the flow of energy. Our thoughts are no different. Positive and negative mean nothing without each other.

In the well-meaning attempt to help, many self-help gurus have implored us to eliminate the negativity from our lives. Stop watching the news. Get rid of negative people. Bludgeon yourself when you have a negative thought until it goes away.

Even if this worked, it would be the lazy way out and leave you without the full experience life has to offer. This attitude of avoidance sets us up for a fall by reducing our world. I'm not proposing that we immerse ourselves in the doom-and-gloom or sky-is-falling rhetoric of the media or indulge our gossiping neighbors with our free time.

I am encouraging the active strengthening of our brains to filter what the world offers and find what we want out of it. Consciously decide what you want for yourself and program your mind to show it to you. That is the only way to enjoy the full scope of this one life.

- If the news doesn't hold anything of value for you, your mind will tune it out and draw you to a more productive activity.
- If a major tragedy in the world can serve to strengthen your mission and deepen your compassion, your mind will tune you in and show you the reason why.

Don't waste your time getting rid of negative thoughts. In doing so, you are still focused on negativity. You become so tuned to the negative that you cannot see the positive that is already there. The focus has to change.

Invest your time looking for what will further your life. Tune your mind to show you opportunity, not limitation. Negativity goes out of focus as a matter of law. It is still there, but no longer your focus or burden.

With all of the Elements of Personal Choice working in your favor, you see what you've asked to see. Your energy isn't devoted to ignoring anything or resisting the idea of negativity. Your energy is targeted and amplified toward the fulfillment of your purposeful vision.

How do I find my life's purpose?

If this question were only about purpose, the preceding chapters would give all the answers needed. Through my own experience and the experiences of thousands of others, I've learned that this question is a case of mistaken identity.

Seeking our life's purpose seems grand and mature. *"It's not that I can't hold a job or commit to a relationship. I'm just trying to find my purpose."*

Finding our life's purpose also seems like the cure to whatever ails us. *"Life seems so pointless. If only I could find my purpose."*

I'm not belittling those feelings at all because they were my feelings too. The feelings are valid, but they aren't fixed with purpose and the answer certainly isn't outside of us. The real question to address the situation is one of awareness and vision. *"What do I want my life to look like?"*

Everyone I have spoken with who asked the purpose question thought they were looking for direction. They didn't realize direction is useless unless you know where you are and where you want to go. Once those are determined, direction can make a difference.

If I hand a compass to someone that is completely lost, they might thank me, but I haven't really done them any good. In a state of panic and depression (lost-ness) any direction seems like an improvement. However, without any navigational reference points you could end up more lost than before. Purpose doesn't help in the absence of awareness and vision.

I have personally tried to establish purpose first and vision second. As long as you're aware of your current location, that can get you started. What I've found is when you take off in a direction without knowing where you want to go, you're likely to waste a lot of energy and become very frustrated. If you have the awareness to establish your vision before your purpose, you can at least take your first stride in the right direction. One without the other negates the effectiveness.

From the department of redundancy department: this is why all seven of the Elements of Personal Choice are necessary. The interplay makes each work. Checks and balances, so to speak. When all of them are in place, they hum and sing to the tune you've determined. If even one is missing, the rest can spin out of control and cause more harm than good.

If you want to ask the question, *"What is my purpose in life?"* I want to encourage you, first establish where you are. Go through the awareness exercise and put a pin in the map. *"This is where I am."* Now go through the vision exercise and decide how you want your life to look. *"This is where I want to go."* Only then can we effectively address purpose.

Why do I procrastinate?

Have you ever wondered why we only hear certain words in one form? Take procrastinate as an example. If there is a pro (in favor of) in the word, I automatically wonder what the word is without the pro. As it turns out, the root word of procrastinate is from the Latin, *crastinium*, meaning tomorrow. So procrastinate means, in favor of tomorrow.

"I could do it today, but I'm in favor of doing it tomorrow." It's easy to see how the word comes to mean, delay. That's the point I want to start with. Procrastinate means to delay or put off action. It is the act of deferment or postponement, not the reason.

When a baseball game is stopped prematurely, they say it is postponed. The reason might be rain or lightning. In other words, postponement isn't the reason for postponement. It's the result of something else. When the something else is handled, the postponement goes away.

For our purposes here, procrastination is the exact same. It is not a cause, but an effect. So why are bookstore shelves full of books that address procrastination like it is the disease? It's like trying to use a band-aid to heal a compound fracture. We have to find the source and treat it there.

Procrastination is the symptom of multiple causes of which you now have the tools to find and treat. Over the years, I have seen every Element of Personal Choice be the root cause of procrastination at one time or another. Let's start at the top and see what rings a bell for you.

Awareness is maybe the easiest to fix. People go unconscious in their pursuit of a goal and simply do not realize they are delaying actions. This is the easiest to fix because as soon as you are aware that you're not taking action, you can.

By making a regular check-in part of your process, you make awareness easier to maintain. The check-in can also help you identify which of the other Elements is causing the delay.

Vision is just as simple to fix, but requires a little more work. How can a lack of vision cause procrastination? If you are unsure of where you are going, you are less likely to make a move. Having a clear vision of your goal attained assures your moves are going to pay off.

Purpose brings additional assurance to your vision. Knowing which steps to take is incredibly useful, but knowing why you are taking them changes the entire landscape. With purpose, we can evaluate a step if unsure. *"This action is in the direction of my vision, but does it also align with my purpose?"* Double reinforcement for added incentive.

Forgiveness is a sneaky cause of procrastination. Most of the forgiveness issues we hold on to do their work out of sight. We collaborate with the resentment or guilt for an internal dialogue that distracts us from the tasks or obstructs our vision from what is really happening.

By identifying and releasing the issues, we have a fog-lifting type of experience. We see things as they are and refocus our attention to what needs completion instead of clouding our thoughts with things already passed.

Action seems obvious since actions are what we delay. The aspect of action I'm referring to though is making sure you're taking the right ones. Remember the Movement Mirage? We can fake ourselves into thinking we are taking action by asking for accountability from others.

This was one of the real revelations for me with the successful people I studied. When they talked about some of their biggest moves and greatest accomplishments, they never mentioned, *"talking to their friends"* as a critical piece of the puzzle. In fact, the whole concept of outside accountability seemed unneeded. Tom, a successful business owner from Texas captured it best.

"If I'm doing something I want to do...why would I need anyone to keep me accountable?"

There's a Mindset Moment for you. If you have gone through all of the steps we've covered together in this book, every action you take serves the purposeful vision of how you want your life to look. Why would you need someone to hold you accountable to doing what it takes to get there? You don't.

Turn up the energy and put it all toward accomplishing what you need. Tell people about your results, not your plans. It's doubtful you'll even have to tell them. Results are typically obvious. If you find yourself seeking outside accountability, take a step back and reassess your goal with the tools available to you now.

The other aspect of the Movement Mirage is talking just because you're excited. I can't fault you on this one. When we get excited, our energy builds to new levels and needs an outlet.

As I covered in the Conquer chapter, when we discuss something with great detail and emotion, or brains get the same rush as when we actually do what were discussing. This is the same pattern we use to our advantage when we bring gratitude into our vision. The difference is in the result.

Gratitude and vision combine to build energy. Talking about our plans depletes energy. You feel like you've done something via an inner action, so it's easier to let outer actions slip. Stay quiet and get something done.

Is it *really* possible for anyone to be successful?

There are dozens of conspiracy theories concerning why success is difficult to attain. The defeatist mantra, *"the rich get richer and the poor get poorer"* makes it seem like you can't have wealth unless you already possess wealth. That notion is complete and total junk.

The idea that people are born for success or have been lucky to get there is a temptation and a trap. If we give in to attributing their success to factors out of our control, we lose. We assume the victim stance and retreat to the safety of mediocrity. The one place success isn't.

My well-reinforced theory as to why people gravitate to *"success being out of their control,"* is they believe it relieves them of responsibility. *"If I don't control my own accomplishments, I can't be held accountable for my lack of effort."*

I've heard thousands of excuses and watched people argue passionately in defense of their unwillingness to go for it. *"Success is for other people and I could never do what they've done because I don't have their advantages."* True failures in life default success to what other people have without considering what success really means.

The way people react to my message of hope, opportunity, and systematic success can be comical, bordering on alarming. Here is an example from a recent conversation after a keynote address.

"So you mean to tell me that I can apply what you're telling me and go have success like Donald Trump?"

"I don't know. Do you define success the same way Trump does? Do you consider him successful?"

"What do you mean? Of course he's successful! He makes billions, has his own TV show..."

"Yes, and is that how YOU define success? Do you have to make billions and have your own TV show to be successful?"

You can see where the conversation is headed. This person made many assumptions regarding success. The biggest is that success is a single place that never moves and is the same for everyone. To become successful we must appreciate that success is relative and dynamic.

Everyone has the right and responsibility to define success on his or her terms. What do you want your life to look like? As I quizzed the Trump fan after the speaking engagement, she admitted that while Trump was financially wealthy and famous, she really didn't know if he was successful in her definition. He seemed lonely and shallow in her estimation.

I reminded her, we don't really know if he is lonely or shallow without knowing him personally and her job wasn't to pursue his success anyway. Her job, and ours, is to define success by our standards and go after our own version. Vision, purpose, belief... they are all individual exercises to begin your trek to success. This is your journey.

The next thing I covered with the Trump fan, and the gathering crowd, was the notion of success being somewhere you arrive and stay. Success is not static.

We define success from where we are at this moment. While we work to reach the goals and milestones we have defined, something else happens. Our view of the world changes and our definition of success expands and changes.

Think of it as progressive horizons. When I stand at the foot of a mountain, all I can think of is getting to the peak. From where I stand, that is what success looks like and is all I can see.

With every step toward that goal, I gain perspective. My elevation changes and new things come into view. As I approach the summit, a new world beyond my current mountain opens up in front of me. I see new horizons and places I would like to go.

This new perspective fuels my desire to explore and experience more. That is the essence of life. Continual growth and exploration makes us appreciative of where we are and excited about where we can go. And as you've probably noticed, this pattern of growth is everything we've discussed in this book.

All of the Elements of Personal Choice are essential climbing companions. We use and reuse each one as we progress through life. As with any other set of tools you use repeatedly, they become easier and more useful the further you go.

Success is absolutely available for everyone. The common trait that you share with all of the truly successful people throughout history is mindset. Using our mindset, we define success, lay the groundwork for achievement, make it happen, and repeat.

Take care of your mindset and it will yield your heart's desires. That is my parting thought.

You've been given the keys to the kingdom. Your understanding of the simple yet immense system that delivers success is beyond anything we have understood before.

With your continued use and mastery of the 7 Elements of Personal Choice, all of the success your heart desires is placed at your fingertips. Your job is to flip the SWITCH.

Are You Ready To Flip Your SWITCH...

And Keep It On?

Stay Connected To PJ

At

www.PJMcClure.com

Made in the USA
San Bernardino, CA
10 June 2016